Law Essentials

COMMERCIAL LAW

Law Essentials

COMMERCIAL LAW

David Cabrelli, LL.B., Dip.L.P.

Solicitor;
Lecturer in Commercial Law,
University of Edinburgh

DUNDEE UNIVERSITY PRESS
2009

First edition published in Great Britain in 2009 by
Dundee University Press
University of Dundee
Dundee DD1 4HN

www.dup.dundee.ac.uk

ISBN 978 1 84586 049 3

No natural forests were destroyed to make this product;
only farmed timber was used and replanted.

British Library Cataloguing-in-Publication Data
A catalogue record for this book is available on request from the British Library

Typeset by Waverley Typesetters, Fakenham
Printed and bound by Bell & Bain Ltd, Glasgow

CONTENTS

TABLE OF CASES

Page

TABLE OF STATUTES

1 SALE OF GOODS

Prior to the enactment of the Sale of Goods Act 1893, the rules on the transfer of title of goods and implied warranties regarding the quality and fitness of goods were regulated by Scots common law. The common law rules were particularly sophisticated and had been developed from civilian principles by the Scots judiciary since the Middle Ages. However, the majority of those rules were abandoned when the Sale of Goods Act 1893 was introduced in the late 19th century. The current law is contained within the Sale of Goods Act 1979 ("the Act").

THE CONTRACT OF SALE

Introduction

Pursuant to s 1(1) of the Act, the coverage of the Act is confined to the contract for the sale of goods which is defined in s 2(1) of the Act as follows:

> "A contract of sale of goods is a contract by which the seller transfers or agrees to transfer the property in the goods to the buyer for a money consideration called the price."

Thus, there are five essential features of the contract of sale of goods, namely: (1) a contract of sale; (2) two parties – a buyer and a seller; (3) the conveyance of property; (4) goods; and (5) the price.

A contract of sale

It is fundamental that a contract must exist between a buyer and a seller. Hence, the usual rules of contract law will apply here, such as the requirements of offer and acceptance and an intention to create legal relations. In terms of s 2(3) of the Act, the contract may be conditional. Thus, the rights and obligations contained in it will require to be performed, and the contract purified, only on the satisfaction of a suspensive condition stipulated in the contract. Where a contract is subject to a suspensive condition or the contract stipulates that the seller will transfer title to the goods at some point in the future, s 2(5) of the Act classifies such a contract as an "agreement to sell". Such an "agreement to sell" is nonetheless covered by the Act.

The contract must be one of "sale". A "sale" is deemed to include a bargain and sale as well as a sale and delivery in terms of s 61(1) of the Act. As a result of this definition, contracts for the exchange of goods (ie goods for goods), which are referred to as "contracts of barter", are not covered by the Act. Scots common law functions to regulate such contracts of barter. Moreover, other contracts which are similar to sale, but which fall outwith the compass of the Act, are credit sale contracts, conditional sale contracts, contracts of hire or hire-purchase contracts. Some of these contracts are controlled by separate regulatory regimes such as the Supply of Goods and Services Act 1982 and the Consumer Credit Act 1974.

A seller and a buyer

Section 61(1) of the Act defines a "seller" as someone who sells or agrees to sell and a "buyer" is a person who buys or agrees to buy goods. Buyers may be consumers or non-consumers. This distinction is important, since the Act provides additional rights to buyers who are classified as consumers. Section 61(1) of the Act directs that a consumer contract is one where one party to the contract deals, and the other party to the contract does not deal or hold himself out as dealing, in the course of a business, and the goods are of a type ordinarily supplied for private use or consumption. However, s 25(1A) of the Unfair Contract Terms Act 1977 ("UCTA") directs that where the consumer is an individual, it is immaterial whether the goods are of a type ordinarily supplied for private use or consumption.

Goods

As for the definition of "goods", one must look to s 61(1) of the Act. Here it is stipulated that "'goods' includes ... all corporeal moveables except money; and in particular 'goods' includes emblements, industrial growing crops, and things attached to or forming part of the land which are agreed to be severed before sale or under the contract of sale and includes an undivided share in goods". This definition has generated some difficulties. For example, contracts for the supply of services do not fall within the compass of the Act. In the case of *Robinson v Graves* (1935), the Court of Appeal ruled that a contract to paint a portrait was a contract for work and labour and not one for the sale of goods. It is unclear whether a contract for the supply of computer software falls within the Act (compare *Beta Computer Systems Europe Ltd v Adobe*

Computer Systems Europe Ltd (1996) with *St Albans DC* v *International Computers Ltd* (1996) and *Erris Promotions Ltd* v *Commissioner of Inland Revenue* (2003)).

Existing goods, future goods, specific goods and unascertained goods

Section 5 of the Act makes a distinction between "existing goods" and "future goods". Existing goods are defined as goods which are "owned or possessed by the seller" at the time of formation of the contract of sale. Meanwhile, "future goods" are goods which are "to be manufactured or acquired by [the seller] after the making of the contract of sale". In the case of future goods, the contract of sale amounts to an agreement to sell. The Act also distinguishes between "specific goods" and "unascertained goods", with the former being defined in s 61(1) of the Act as "goods identified and agreed on at the time a contract of sale is made ... includ[ing] an undivided share, specified as a fraction or percentage, of goods identified and agreed on as aforesaid", whereas unascertained goods are goods which are neither so identified or agreed. It is not possible to have a contract to sell unascertained goods by virtue of s 16 of the Act – only an agreement to sell unascertained goods. However, an exception applies in the case of s 20A of the Act, where the contract is to sell unascertained goods which form part of an identified bulk, eg an earmarked crop of potatoes forming part of a larger bulk.

Price

Section 8 of the Act stipulates that the price may be fixed by the contract, may be left to be fixed in a manner agreed by the contract, or may be determined by the course of dealing between the parties. However, where such factors are not determinative of matters, s 8(2) and (3) of the Act state that the buyer must pay a reasonable price and a reasonable price is fact dependent. In the case of *Glynwed Distribution Ltd* v *S Koronka & Co Ltd* (1977), it was held that a reasonable price will be a price which is fair and just to the relevant parties to the contract – not necessarily the open market price.

TIME

In terms of s 10 of the Act, subject to contrary agreement, stipulations as to time of payment are not of the essence in a contract of sale.

PASSING OF PROPERTY

Introduction

The Scots common law of sale of goods provided that the transfer of title from the seller to the buyer required the delivery of the goods and the will or intention of the seller to transfer. Delivery could be physical, constructive or symbolic. The common law position can be contrasted with s 17(1) of the Act which stipulates that where there is a contract for the sale of specific or ascertained goods the property in them is transferred to the buyer at such time as the parties to the contract intend it to be transferred. Thus, title to property passes with intention and intention is to be ascertained from the contract of sale. Where the intention of the parties cannot be ascertained, there are five rules contained in s 18 of the Act which provide guidance.

The five rules

Rule 1 of s 18 of the Act stipulates that where there is an unconditional contract for the sale of specific goods in a deliverable state the property in the goods passes to the buyer when the contract is made. Thus, provided the goods are specific in the sense described in s 61(1) of the Act so that they are earmarked, title to the property will pass when an unconditional contract of sale is concluded despite the fact that delivery or payment of the price has not yet been made. Section 61(5) of the Act states that the goods are deemed to be in a "deliverable state" where the buyer would, under the contract, be bound to take delivery of them. Subject to an exception which applies in the case of ss 20A and 20B of the Act, s 61(5) provides that the word "delivery" denotes a "voluntary transfer of possession from one person to another".

Rule 2 directs that if something requires to be done to place specific goods into a state whereby the purchaser would be bound under the contract to take delivery, property will not pass in those goods until that thing is done. Here, one can envisage circumstances such as setting aside goods in sacks, bags or on pallets. Rule 3 takes the point a little further by stating that where goods require to be weighed, measured, tested, or some other act or thing needs to be done with reference to the goods for the purpose of ascertaining the price, the property does not pass until the act or thing is done and the buyer has notice that it has been done.

Rule 4 goes on to cover goods delivered to the purchaser on approval or on sale or return. Here, title to the goods is deemed to pass to the purchaser (i) when the purchaser signifies his approval or acceptance to the seller or does any other act adopting the transaction, or (ii) if the purchaser does not signify his approval or acceptance to the seller but retains the goods without giving notice of rejection, then, if a time has been fixed for the return of the goods, on the expiration of that time, or, if no time has been fixed, on the expiration of a reasonable notice.

Finally, rule 5 is drawn in terms of four segments and only the first will be dealt with here. It is to the effect that where there is a contract for the sale of unascertained or future goods by description, and goods of that description and in a deliverable state are unconditionally appropriated to the contract, either by the seller with the express or implied assent of the buyer or by the buyer with the assent of the seller, the property in the goods then passes to the buyer. In the case of *Carlos Federspiel & Co SA* v *Charles Twigg & Co Ltd* (1957), Pearson J remarked that in order to constitute an appropriation of the goods to the contract, the parties must have had, or be reasonably supposed to have had, an intention to attach the contract irrevocably to those goods, so that those goods and no others are the subject of the sale and become the property of the buyer.

Reservation of title

As a logical consequence of the rule that the property to the goods passes when the parties intend it to pass, s 19(1) of the Act empowers the seller to reserve the right of disposal of the goods until certain conditions are fulfilled. Thus, a seller may stipulate that title is reserved in favour of the seller, notwithstanding delivery of the goods to the purchaser. The most obvious reason a seller might wish to retain title to the goods is to ensure that he receives payment from the purchaser. A contractual term called a "reservation of title clause" will achieve this. Here, property does not pass in the goods and remains with the seller until the purchaser pays the purchase price to the seller in full.

There are two kinds of retention of title clause, namely (1) the clause which provides that title will only pass to the purchaser once the price for those goods has been paid in full to the seller, and (2) the clause which provides that title will only pass to the purchaser once the price for those goods and all sums owing (in terms of other transactions) to the seller have been paid in full to the seller. The insertion of the first form of this clause simply renders a contract of sale subject to a suspensive condition and causes no difficulty for the Scottish courts, eg see *Archivent Sales & Development Ltd* v *Strathclyde RC* (1985). However, the second form of clause known as an "all sums" clause was initially struck down by the

Scottish courts as an attempt to create a security over corporeal moveables without possession in the case of *Deutz Engines Ltd* v *Terex Ltd* (1984). However, in the case of *Armour* v *Thyssen Edelstahlwerke AG* (1990), the House of Lords (on appeal from the Court of Session) ruled that such "all sums" clauses were valid and simply another means of applying the rules in ss 17 and 19 of the Act.

Third party rights

The rights of third parties to property are also covered in the Act. Section 21 of the Act governs the situation where goods are sold by a non-owner. At the heart of the law lies a tension between the principle that someone's property rights should be protected (ie that an owner of goods should not be deprived of title where a third party purports to sell those goods to a buyer) and the principle that commercial transactions should be safeguarded (ie that a person who takes property from a non-owner of those goods in good faith and for value without notice should obtain a good title). The general rule in s 21(1) states that where goods are sold by a person who is not their owner, without the authority or the consent of the owner, the buyer acquires no better title to the goods than the seller had, unless the owner of the goods is by his conduct precluded from denying the seller's authority to sell. This is the Act's way of articulating the classic principle *nemo dat quod non habet* which seeks to protect the property rights of the owner of the goods, ie that no one can pass a better title than that which he had.

However, there are exceptions to this general rule which seek to protect buyers of goods. The first exception is contained in the latter part of s 21(1) and applies where the real owner of the goods has taken action which personally bars him from challenging the non-owner's right to sell. The second exception is governed by s 24(1) of the Act. In terms of s 24(1) of the Act, if A sells goods to B but retains physical possession of the goods and then sells those same goods to C, C will take title to the goods provided C is in good faith and has no notice of the prior sale to B. The third exception is contained in s 25(1) of the Act and builds on s 24(1) of the Act by providing that a buyer in possession of goods which are still owned by a seller may give good title to those goods to a third party purchaser, provided that third party purchaser is in good faith and has no notice of the rights of the seller in the goods. So if A relinquishes possession of goods to B pursuant to a contract of sale and title remains with A, B nevertheless may confer good title on C where C buys the goods from B, provided C is in good faith and has no notice of the rights of A. Section 25(1) of the Act can operate to defeat a seller's rights under a retention of title clause which they have included in a contract of sale. However, in the case of *National Employers Mutual General Insurance Association Ltd* v *Jones* (1990), it was decided that s 25 of the Act does not function to enable a seller A who did not have title to the goods to confer good title on C, eg where A had stolen the goods from Z.

Section 23 of the Act sets out the rule that where a seller has a voidable title to goods, but it has not been avoided at the time of sale, the buyer obtains a good title provided he acts in good faith and without notice of the defect in title. Moreover, even after the buyer's title has been avoided, the buyer in possession may be able to pass good title under s 25. Finally, s 2(1) of the Factors Act 1889 states that where a mercantile agent is in possession of goods or of the documents of title to goods with the consent of the owner, any sale of the goods made by him in the ordinary course of business will be sufficient to confer good title on a third party purchaser, provided that third party acts in good faith, and has no notice that the mercantile agent has no authority to sell the goods.

PASSING OF RISK

Introduction

The parties have the power to include a provision in their contract of sale which specifies when the risk of damage or destruction of goods passes from the seller to the purchaser. Where the parties fail to agree when risk is to pass, the Act provides certain default rules which will apply. Section 20(1) of the Act is to the effect that the goods remain at the seller's risk until title is transferred to the buyer and that once title is transferred to the buyer the goods are at the buyer's risk whether delivery has been made or not. Section 20(2) of the Act goes on to state that where delivery has been delayed through the fault of either buyer or seller, the goods are at the risk of the party at fault as regards any loss which might not have occurred but for such fault. A good example of this principle is provided by the case of *Demby Hamilton & Co Ltd* v *Barden* (1949) where the buyer delayed in providing instructions as to the delivery of apple juice in casks. The apple juice went "off" and the delay of the buyer was used as a justification for the risk of deterioration to rest with the buyer although title in the goods remained with the seller.

Exception to general rule

However, a major exception to the general rule is provided in s 20(4) of the Act which stipulates that, where there is a consumer contract, the goods remain at the seller's risk until they are delivered to the consumer. It is not possible to disapply this rule in the contract for the sale of goods between the consumer and the seller.

THE SELLER'S DUTIES

Introduction

The Act imposes a number of duties on the seller of goods. There are two principal duties.

Delivery

First, the seller must deliver the goods to the purchaser. The relevant rules are included in ss 27–30 of the Act. Section 61 of the Act defines delivery as "the voluntary transfer of possession from one person to another" rather than physical delivery of the goods.

Goods conform to contract of sale

The second principal duty of the seller is to provide goods which are conform to the contract of sale. The contract of sale is comprised of express terms agreed by the parties and implied terms which are imposed into the parties' contract of sale by the Act. These implied terms are specified in ss 12–15 of the Act and confer a great degree of protection in favour of purchasers.

Implied term as to title

Section 12(1) of the Act stipulates that, subject to one particular exception, it is an implied term of a contract of sale that the seller has a right to sell the goods, and in the case of an agreement to sell that he will have such a right at the time when the property is to pass. Subsection (2) of s 12 goes on to provide that there is an implied term of the contract of sale that (i) the goods are free, and will remain free until the time when the property is to pass, from any charge or encumbrance not disclosed or known to the buyer before the contract is made, and (ii) the buyer will enjoy quiet possession of the goods except so far as it may be disturbed by the owner or other person entitled to the benefit of any charge or encumbrance so disclosed or known. Thus if a seller purports to transfer title to goods where he does not have the right to sell them, the seller will be in breach of the contract of sale. However, where the seller's title to the goods or right to sell them is perfected subsequent to the sale, this will operate to cure the breach (eg *Butterworth* v *Kingsway Motors Ltd* (1954)).

Consequences of breach of implied term as to title

Where the seller breaches the implied term to give good title to the goods in s 12(1) of the Act, in terms of ss 15B(1) and 53A of the Act, the buyer's remedies are rejection of the goods and return of the price or damages. Additional remedies are available where the contract of sale is a consumer contract in terms of ss 15B(2), 48A, 48B and 48C of the Act (see below under "The buyer's remedies").

Implied term as to sale by description

Section 13(1) of the Act narrates that where there is a contract for the sale of goods by description, there is an implied term that the goods will correspond with the description. All online sales are deemed as a sale by description. A sale by description may be in images or numbers (eg *Beale* v *Taylor* (1967)).

Although the word "description" covers words, images and numbers, it is insufficiently wide in scope to cover the capacity or power of the goods in the absence of an express specification (eg *Border Harvesters Ltd* v *Edwards Engineering (Perth) Ltd* (1985)).

Implied term as to satisfactory quality

Section 14(2) of the Act stipulates that where the goods are sold in the course of a business, there is an implied term that the goods supplied will be of satisfactory quality. The requirement that sales must be in the course of a business has been interpreted liberally, so that it is only purely private sales which fall outwith this definition. In terms of s 14(2A) of the Act, goods are deemed to be of satisfactory quality if they meet the standard that a reasonable person would regard as satisfactory, taking account of any description of the goods, the price (if relevant) and all the other relevant circumstances. Section 14(2D) complements s 14(2A) by stating that if a contract of sale is a consumer contract the relevant circumstances mentioned in s 14(2A) of the Act include any public statements on the specific characteristics of the goods made about them by the seller, the producer or his representative, particularly in advertising or on labelling. Section 14(2B) of the Act goes on to provide that the quality of goods includes their state and condition and the following (among others) are in appropriate cases aspects of the quality of goods:

(a) fitness for all the purposes for which goods of the kind in question are commonly supplied;

(b) appearance and finish;

(c) freedom from minor defects;

(d) safety; and

(e) durability.

The implied term in s 14(2C) of the Act does not apply to any defect which is specifically drawn to the buyer's attention before the contract is made and, where the buyer examines the goods before the contract is made, the implied term does not cover any defect which that examination ought to reveal. As for how "satisfactory quality" is to be assessed, the cases of *Clegg* v *Andersson* (2003) and *Jewson Ltd* v *Boyhan* (2004) demonstrate that it is to be considered from the standpoint of the hypothetical reasonable person (which does not involve any assumption of expertise) and the assessment varies according to the nature of the goods and the persons to which it is targeted.

The five factors Section 14(2B) of the Act lists five pertinent factors. The first factor, namely "fitness for all the purposes for which goods of the kind in question are commonly supplied" overlaps with the separate statutory implied term of "fitness for a particular purpose" set out in s 14(3) of the Act. The standard of "all common purposes" in s 14(2B)(a) of the Act is a very high standard for the seller to discharge and so if goods are not fit for one of the purposes for which they are usually supplied, then the seller must make this fact known to the buyer. With regard to "appearance and finish" in s 14(2B)(b) of the Act, shoddy workmanship in appearance and finish will be treated as a breach of the "satisfactory quality" implied term regardless of the sophistication, price and/or specification (or otherwise) of the goods. Section 14(2B)(c) of the Act narrates that goods must be free from minor defects. For example, in the case of *Lamarra* v *Capital Bank plc* (2006), a Range Rover had a number of minor defects, namely when driven the vehicle pulled to the left causing undue tyre wear, the layout of the pedals was faulty, there was a loud noise from the engine or transmission system, there was a deep scratch on the ashtray, the glove box was incorrectly fitted, the paintwork on parts of the roof was poorly finished and the navigation disc was missing. It was held that the Range Rover was not free from minor defects and so the statutory implied term of satisfactory quality had been breached. Moreover, the court stated that the reasonableness or otherwise of the buyer's conduct cannot be relevant to the determination of satisfactory quality. However, the court did say that the implied term of satisfactory quality and the factor of freedom from minor defects do not entitle a purchaser in law to expect perfection in the goods supplied. *Lamarra* can be contrasted quite sharply with the decisions in the earlier cases of *Millars of Falkirk* v *Turpie* (1976) and *Bernstein* v *Pamson Motors (Golders Green) Ltd* (1987) where the attitude of the judiciary was to the effect that the law expected buyers of motor vehicles simply to put up with minor defects. It is likely that the courts would follow *Lamarra* in modern times.

The final component of the seller's duty to provide goods of a satisfactory quality is contained in s 14(2B)(d) and (e) of the Act. Here, it is stipulated that goods must be safe and durable. In relation to the criterion of durability, the case of *Thain* v *Anniesland Trade Centre* (1997) is a cause for concern for purchasers of second-hand vehicles. Here, it was ruled that durability was not a quality reasonably to be expected of a second-hand car where a faulty gear box rendered the car a write-off 2 weeks subsequent to its purchase.

Implied term of fitness for purpose

Section 14(3) of the Act complements s 14(2) by providing that goods supplied must be reasonably fit for the particular purpose to which they are to be put where this is made known to the seller by the purchaser (expressly or by implication), whether or not that is a purpose for which such goods are commonly supplied, except where the circumstances show that the buyer does not rely, or that it is unreasonable for him to rely, on the skill or judgement of the seller or credit-broker. In *Jewson Ltd* v *Boyhan* (2004), the court clarified the respective roles of s 14(3) and (2B)(a) of the Act. The former is relevant to impose a particular obligation tailored to the particular circumstances of a particular case, whereas the latter serves to impose an obligation on a seller for breach of the duty to provide goods of satisfactory quality where the purpose for which the goods are to be used is a common purpose. A final point to make is that goods will not be deemed to be unfit for purpose where, due to an idiosyncrasy in the buyer or the buyer's property, there would appear to be a defect in the goods. For example, in the case of *Griffiths* v *Peter Conway Ltd* (1939), it was held that a Harris tweed coat was not defective where the purchaser contracted dermatitis by wearing it and it could be proven that the purchaser had abnormally sensitive skin. If the coat had been worn by a person with normal skin, it was clear that no dermatitis would have been contracted by that person.

Implied term as to sales by sample

The final implied term of the contract of sale is set out in s 15 of the Act. Section 15(2)(a) and (c) of the Act provide that, in the case of a contract for sale by sample, there is an implied term that (i) the bulk must correspond to the sample in quality and (ii) the goods must be free from any defect which renders their quality unsatisfactory, which would not be apparent on a reasonable examination of the sample. Section 15(1) of the Act stipulates that a contract of sale is a contract for sale by sample where there is an express or implied term to that effect in the contract.

THE BUYER'S REMEDIES

Where the seller has breached one of the statutory duties in terms of ss 13–15 of the Act or one of the express terms of the contract of sale, there are a number of options available to the buyer, depending on whether the contract of sale is a consumer contract or non-consumer contract, as the case may be. Where the buyer is a consumer, there are additional remedies which are apparent from the following table summarising the main remedies:

Status of buyer	Remedy
Non-consumer	Right to damages – s 15B(1) of the Act.
Non-consumer	Right to rescind and reject all of the goods if the breach is material – s 15B(1)(b) of the Act. In *Clegg v Andersson* (2003), it was ruled that a buyer has a free choice to seek damages or rejection as he pleases.
Non-consumer	Right to accept some of the goods and reject some of the goods if some of the goods are not in conformity with the contract of sale – s 35A(1) of the Act.
Non-consumer	Right to an order of specific implement where the seller has breached his obligation to deliver specific or ascertained goods – s 52(1) of the Act.

Status of buyer	Remedy
Consumer	Right to damages – s 15B(1) of the Act.
Consumer	Right to rescind and reject the goods if the breach is material – s 15B(2) of the Act. A breach of the statutory implied terms in ss 13–15 of the Act is deemed to be a material breach of contract if the buyer is a consumer – 15B(2) of the Act.
Consumer	Right to accept some of the goods and reject some of the goods if some of the goods are not in conformity with the contract of sale – s 35A(1) of the Act.
Consumer	Right to an order of specific implement where the seller has breached his obligation to deliver specific or ascertained goods – s 52(1) of the Act.
Consumer	Right to have the goods repaired or replaced – s 48B(1)(a) and (b) of the Act.
Consumer	Right to require the seller to reduce the purchase price of the goods by an appropriate amount, or rescind the contract with regard to those goods where (a) the buyer may require neither repair nor replacement of the goods due to the impossibility or disproportionality of repair or replacement, or (b) the buyer has required the seller to repair or replace the goods, but the seller is in breach of the requirement to repair or replace within a reasonable time and without significant inconvenience to the buyer – s 48C(1) and (2) of the Act.

Measure of damages

Sections 51(2) and 53A(1) of the Act stipulate that the measure of the buyer's damages on a breach of an express or implied term of the contract of sale (in terms of s 15B(1) of the Act) is the estimated loss directly and naturally arising, in the ordinary course of events, from the seller's breach – whether the goods were delivered or not. Where an action is raised for damages on non-delivery of the goods and there is an available market for the goods, s 51(3) of the Act states that the measure of damages is prima facie to be ascertained by the difference between the contract price and the market or current price of the goods at the time or times when they ought to have been delivered or, if no time was fixed, at the time of the refusal to deliver. Where the goods are delivered and are defective, how this is calculated depends on whether the buyer rejects or retains the defective goods. If the buyer rejects the defective goods, damages will be calculated on the basis that the goods have not been delivered, ie in terms of s 51(3) set out above. However, s 53A(2) of the Act provides that if the buyer retains the defective goods, the damages will be the difference between the value of the goods at the time of delivery and their value had the contract been fulfilled.

The buyer's right of rejection

A buyer will have lost the right to reject when he has accepted the goods or is deemed to have accepted the goods. Section 35(1) of the Act provides that the buyer is deemed to have accepted the goods when intimation is given to the seller to that effect or when he takes delivery of the goods and does any act in relation to them which is inconsistent with ownership remaining with the seller (see *Fiat Auto Financial Services* v *Connelly* (2007)). In terms of s 35(2) of the Act, the buyer is not deemed to have accepted the goods where he has not previously examined them until he has had a reasonable opportunity of examining them for the purpose of ascertaining whether they conform to the contract of sale and, in the case of contract for sale by sample, of comparing the bulk with the sample. In the case of *Henry Pini & Co to George Smith & Co* (1895), it was ruled that it is likely that once the reasonable opportunity to examine has passed the right to reject will be lost. The buyer is also deemed to have accepted the goods when, after the lapse of a reasonable time, he retains the goods without intimating to the seller that he has rejected them.

For further guidance on what constitutes a reasonable period of time, one must look to the case law. However, the difficulty with it is that it paints no clear picture as to what period of time is "reasonable" and much depends on the nature of the goods acquired (see *Bernstein* v *Pamson Motors (Golders Green) Ltd* [1987] 2 All ER 220 at 230h–j), the balancing of the opposing interests of the buyer and seller (see *Truk (UK) Ltd* v *Tokmakidis GmbH* [2000] 1 Lloyd's Rep 543 at 550, per Raymond Jack J), the whole circumstances of the case and other factors. For example, in the case of *Bernstein* v *Pamson Motors (Golders Green) Ltd*

(1987) a period of 3 weeks in the case of the purchase of a new Nissan Laurel motor car (140 miles having been clocked up) was held not to be a reasonable period of time and accordingly it was held that the right of rejection had been lost. *Bernstein* can be contrasted with *Rogers* v *Parish (Scarborough) Ltd* (1987), where it was held that a purchaser had not lost his right to reject when it rejected a Range Rover motor vehicle 6 months subsequent to the date of purchase and had clocked up in excess of 5,500 miles in that period. A similar approach was adopted in *Truk (UK) Ltd* v *Tokmakidis GmbH* (2000) where the purchasers of a chassis and underlift were entitled to reject 7 months after the date of conclusion of the contract.

Section 35(6) of the Act provides further guidance with regard to the expiry of the buyer's right to reject. Here, it is stated that a buyer does not lose his right to reject merely because the seller and buyer have agreed to the repair the goods. Where the goods are repaired, but the seller refuses to disclose the nature of the defect to the buyer, *J & H Ritchie Ltd* v *Lloyd Ltd* (2007) decided that the buyer did not lose his right to reject the repaired machinery subsequently even though the seller refused to disclose the nature of the defect and limited disclosure to informing the buyer that the goods had been repaired to "factory gate specification". A consumer cannot lose his right to inspect the goods by waiver or otherwise in terms of s 35(3) of the Act.

Consumer remedies

Finally, where a buyer is a consumer, further remedies are available. In terms of s 48B(1) and (2) of the Act, the consumer has the right to have the goods repaired or replaced by the seller within a reasonable period of time without causing significant inconvenience to the consumer and the seller must bear any necessary costs incurred in doing so (including in particular the cost of any labour, materials or postage). Section 61(1) of the Act stipulates that repair means that modifications must be made to bring the goods into conformity with the contract. However, a buyer is relieved of the obligation to repair or replace where the remedy is impossible, where the grant of one remedy (eg repair) would be disproportionate in comparison to the other (eg replacement) and where either remedy would be disproportionate to the other remedies available under s 48C of the Act, namely reduction in price, or rescission.

The consumer may seek to invoke the remedy of rescission or the reduction of the purchase price of the goods in terms of s 48C of the

Act. However, s 48C(2) stipulates that these remedies are subsidiary to the remedies of repair or replacement. Thus, a buyer may only seek rescission or a reduction of the price if he is unable to compel the seller to repair or replace the goods on the grounds of impossibility, that repair or replacement is disproportionate or in the case of a breach on the part of the seller to repair or replace within a reasonable time and without significant inconvenience to the buyer.

THE BUYER'S DUTIES

The duties of the buyer are threefold in terms of the Act. First, to accept the goods. Secondly, to pay the price in accordance with the contract of sale in terms of s 27 of the Act. In terms of s 10 of the Act, time is not usually of the essence in contracts of sale. The effect of this rule is that the seller will not have the right to rescind if payment is not made timeously. Finally, the buyer is under a duty to take delivery of the goods within a reasonable period of time in terms of s 37 of the Act.

THE SELLER'S REMEDIES

Notwithstanding the fact that ownership of the goods has passed to the buyer, s 39(1) of the Act provides that the seller is entitled to exercise the following possessory remedies when he has not been paid:

- a lien on the goods or a right to retain them for the price while he is in possession of them;
- in the case of the insolvency of the buyer, a right of stopping the goods in transit after he has parted with the possession of them; and/or
- a right of re-sale.

Essential Facts

- A contract of sale of goods is a contract by which the seller transfers or agrees to transfer the property in the goods to the buyer for a money consideration called the price.
- The word "goods" includes all corporeal moveables except money, emblements, industrial growing crops, and things attached to or forming part of the land which are agreed to be severed before sale

or under the contract of sale and includes an undivided share in goods.

- Where there is a contract for the sale of specific or ascertained goods the property in them is transferred to the buyer at such time as the parties to the contract intend it to be transferred.

- Where the intention of the parties cannot be ascertained, there are five rules contained in s 18 of the Act which determine whether title to the goods has passed.

- The goods remain at the seller's risk until title is transferred to the buyer and once title is transferred to the buyer the goods are at the buyer's risk whether delivery has been made or not.

- The seller must provide goods which are conform to the contract of sale.

- The seller must comply with the statutory implied terms.

- Where the seller breaches an express term or one of the statutory implied terms, the buyer will have a right to damages, a right to rescind and reject all of the goods if the breach is material, the right to accept some of the goods and reject some of the goods and the right to obtain a decree of specific implement.

- A consumer has additional remedies, namely a right to have the goods repaired or replaced, a right to require the seller to reduce the purchase price of the goods by an appropriate amount and/ or the right to rescind the contract where repair or replacement is impossible, disproportionate or cannot be achieved within a reasonable time.

- A buyer will have lost the right to reject when he has accepted the goods or is deemed to have accepted the goods.

Essential Cases

Robinson v Graves (1935): a contract to paint a portrait was a contract for work and labour and not one for the sale of goods.

Beale v Taylor (1967): a car advertised by model and year was sufficient to constitute a sale by description.

Clegg v Andersson (2003) and **Jewson Ltd v Boyhan (2004)**: "satisfactory quality" is to be considered from the standpoint of the hypothetical reasonable person and the assessment varies according to the nature of the goods and the persons to which it is targeted.

Lamarra v Capital Bank plc (2006): where a Range Rover had minor defects, it was held that the statutory implied term of satisfactory quality had been breached.

Thain v Anniesland Trade Centre (1997): durability was not a quality reasonably to be expected of a second-hand car where a faulty gear box rendered the car a write-off 2 weeks subsequent to its purchase.

Fiat Auto Financial Services v Connelly (2007): a buyer's continued use of a vehicle as a taxi for several months did not amount to acts inconsistent with ownership of the seller where the buyer was liaising with the seller regularly with regard to concerns over the vehicle's fitness for purpose.

Henry Pini & Co v George Smith & Co (1895): it is likely that once the reasonable opportunity to examine the goods has passed, the right of the buyer to reject the goods will be lost.

Bernstein v Pamson Motors (Golders Green) Ltd (1987): where the purchaser of a new Nissan Laurel motor car (140 miles having been clocked up) attempted to reject the goods after a period of 3 weeks, this was held not to be a reasonable period of time within which to reject.

Rogers v Parish (Scarborough) Ltd (1987): it was ruled that a purchaser had not lost his right to reject when he rejected a Range Rover motor vehicle (which had clocked up in excess of 5,500 miles) 6 months subsequent to the date of purchase.

Truk (UK) Ltd. v Tokmakidis GmbH (2000): held that the purchasers of a chassis and underlift were entitled to reject 7 months after the date of conclusion of the contract.

J & H Ritchie Ltd v Lloyd Ltd (2007): a buyer did not lose his right to reject repaired machinery where the seller refused to disclose the nature of the defect and limited disclosure to informing the buyer that the goods had been repaired to "factory gate specification".

2 HIRE

A contract of hire is one form of a contract of location (Stair, *Institutions*, I, 15, 1). Certain implied terms in law are incorporated into every contract of hire by the common law and ss 11G–11L of the Supply of Goods and Services Act 1982 ("the 1982 Act"), much in the same way as certain implied terms in law are implied into every contract for the sale of goods by virtue of the Sale of Goods Act 1979.

TYPES OF HIRE CONTRACT

Finance lease

There are a number of modern forms of the contract of hire. The first is the finance lease, where a lessee selects goods from a supplier and the lessor purchases those goods from the supplier and hires them to the lessee for a specific period in return for rental payments. Thus, the lessor acts as purchaser vis-à-vis the supplier and lessor vis-à-vis the lessee. To that extent, the lessor acts as financier and the rental payments cover the lessor's aggregate capital costs of providing the goods to the lessee, the lessor's expenses and a margin in respect of the lessor's profit for acting as financier.

Operating lease

In the case of an operating lease, the lessor assumes some of the risk that the value of the equipment let to the lessee will be inadequate at the end of the lease to enable the lessor to recoup his investment in the equipment. This is the case, since the rentals of the lessee and the capital allowances available to the lessee in respect of the equipment will be such that they do not represent sufficient funds to redeem the cost of that investment.

Contract hire

Another type of contract of hire is contract hire. Contract hire is usually encountered in the context of the hire of commercial vehicles. In terms of this contract, a finance house will let a vehicle to an employer for 3 years for use by the employees. The rent is pitched at a level which is sufficient to cover the acquisition cost of the car or vehicle minus the estimated residual value of the car or vehicle to the finance house at the termination of the 3-year period.

Rental or hire agreement

The rental or hire agreement is often used in respect of consumer goods. The rental or hire agreement may endure for a short- or long-term period, depending on the nature of the equipment. The owner/lessor will commonly provide various warranties as to the condition and fitness for purpose of the goods and also provide maintenance and servicing assistance. To that extent, the owner/lessor will maintain some responsibility towards the hirer in respect of the proper functioning of those goods.

THE ESSENTIALS OF THE CONTRACT OF HIRE

Stair stipulates that there are three essential elements to the contract of hire, namely a thing to be let, a passing rent agreed upon and finally the consent of the contracting parties (Stair, *Institutions*, I, 15, 1). To these three requirements, Bell adds a fourth factor, namely a specified period of let (Bell, *Commentaries*, I, 481). Any moveables may qualify as the thing let, so long as the nature of the goods is such that they are not consumable. The passing rent should be in money, rather than money's worth. However, in the case of *Wilson* v *Orr* (1879), the Court of Session was content to classify the hire of a horse in return for a rent comprised of providing the horse's keep as a contract of hire. The final requisite factor, namely the consent of the contracting parties, may manifest itself verbally or in writing. However, where the contract of hire qualifies as a consumer hire agreement in terms of the Consumer Credit Act 1974 ("the 1974 Act"), ss 60 and 61 of the 1974 Act direct that the agreement must be reduced to writing and the lessor must possess a licence under that Act.

COMMON LAW IMPLIED TERMS

Introduction

The implied terms of the contract of hire can be conceptualised as imposing obligations on the lessor and the lessee and conferring reciprocal rights in favour of the same. These implied terms are sometimes referred to as the *naturalia* of the contract of hire.

Lessor's common law obligations

First, we will consider the common law implied terms which impose obligations on the lessor.

Duty to deliver

The first implied term to mention is the lessor's duty to deliver the subjects of hire in a state of good condition and repair (*Wilson* v *Norris* (1810)). The expenses of delivery must be borne by the lessor. The doctrine of *rei interitus* applies to the contract for the hire of goods in much the same way as the contract for the lease of heritage. That is to say that where the subjects of hire are destroyed and delivery is no longer possible, the hirer will no longer wield the right to force the lessor to render such delivery.

Duty not to interfere

Secondly, the lessor must not interfere with the lessee's enjoyment of the subjects of hire and warrants against such interference. The rationale behind this rule is that the lessor must not impede the lessee's enjoyment of the thing hired. To that extent, the lessor warrants his title to the goods. However, where possession is lost by the lessee as a result of the lessor breaching his warranty against such interference, the effect is that the contract of hire is terminated, no further rent is payable by the lessee and the lessee is entitled to claim damages from the lessor.

Duty to keep goods in good order and repair

Thirdly, the lessor has a duty to keep the goods hired in sufficiently good order and repair. The purpose of this implied term is to ensure that the lessee has the ability to continue to use the goods hired throughout the period of hire. Some minor repairs must be borne, however, by the lessee: eg in the case of the hire of a vehicle, the lessee will be under an obligation to change the tyres and meet the cost of doing so. During the period that the goods are undergoing repair and the lessee does not have use of the goods, the lessee will be entitled to an abatement of rent. However, there are exceptions to this rule: eg where a car breaks down where it is subject to a long-term hire contract, the rent will probably not be subject to an abatement (*Wilson* v *Norris* (1810)).

Warranty as to good title

Finally, the common law provides that the lessor is under an obligation to warrant that the goods let are free from defects, ie that the goods are fit for ordinary uses and purposes or for any particular uses in the contemplation of the parties. However, it is subject to doubt whether the lessor is under continuing liability for latent defects. Bell's *Principles*, s 141 states that there is no continuing liability for latent defects where the lessor was unaware of them or could not reasonably have known of them. However, in *Wilson* v *Norris* (1810), the opposite view was taken.

Exception for finance leases and operating leases

Where the contract of hire qualifies as a finance lease or operating lease, the contract will be treated as a *sui generis* contract (ie not as a contract of hire) and so the above implied term that the lessor has a good unencumbered title to the goods will not be implied into those contracts (*G M Shepherd Ltd* v *North West Securities Ltd* (1991)). That is, where a finance lessor is not involved in the selection of the hired goods, the contract will not amount to the nominate contract of hire and so the implied term that the lessor has a duty to warrant that the goods let are free from defects will not apply. However, whether the result of *G M Shepherd* is that all of the implied terms of the contract of hire do not apply to the finance lease or operating lease is not particularly clear.

Lessee's common law obligations

There are essentially five common law obligations imposed on a lessee.

Duty to take delivery

The lessee is under an obligation to take delivery of the goods hired. Where the lessee breaches this obligation, the lessor is entitled to seek damages and terminate the contract. The alternative remedy is specific implement.

Duty to pay rent

Secondly, the lessee must pay the rent. Usually, the rent will be paid in arrears. However, the contract or custom may provide or indicate otherwise. Subject to exceptions, where the lessee is temporarily deprived of the use and enjoyment of the thing hired, he will have the right to a rent abatement.

Duty to use the goods for the purpose for which they were let

Thirdly, there is an implied term to the effect that the lessee must use the goods hired for the purpose for which they were let. In the case of *Seton* v *Paterson* (1880) where a horse was hired for the purpose of undertaking a day's journey, but it was taken for a gallop race by the lessee, the lessee was held to be in breach of this implied term. The same point would apply to cars in modern times.

Duty to take proper care of the goods

Fourthly, the lessee is under a duty to take proper care of the goods hired (Stair, *Institutions*, I, 15, 5). The lessee is not liable for casual or accidental perishing of the goods hired. In *Campbell* v *Lord Kennedy* (1828) the lessee of a horse was deemed to be in breach of the implied term where he lent it to a friend whose actions resulted in the horse catching a chill and dying. However, if the goods deteriorate due to fair wear and tear or the goods are damaged as a result of something which was not the lessee's fault, the lessee will not have breached this implied term. If the goods perish in circumstances which were not the fault of the lessee, the lessor must take the risk of such destruction (*Jacksons (Edinburgh) Ltd* v *Constructors John Brown Ltd* (1965)).

Duty to restore the thing hired in a good state of condition and repair

Finally, the lessee has a duty to restore the thing hired to the lessor in a good state of condition and repair. This implied term complements the implied term that the lessee is under a duty to take proper care of the goods hired during the period of hire. As explained by Lord Justice-Clerk Moncrieff in *Wilson* v *Orr* (1879), if the lessee is able to discharge the latter implied term, he will stand in good stead for the purposes of the implied term of restoring the thing let in good condition towards the end of the period of hire. Of course, where damage is caused to the goods which was not his fault, the lessee is not liable to the lessor, provided he is able to justify and explain the loss. Where the lessee cannot explain or justify the loss, he will be liable to the lessor for the value of the goods lost.

STATUTORY REGULATION OF THE CONTRACT OF HIRE

Consumer hire agreements

Where a contract of hire qualifies as a consumer hire agreement in terms of s 15(1) of the 1974 Act, the lessor will require a consumer credit licence under Part III of that Act before entering into such an agreement. The agreement must be set out in writing by virtue of ss 60 and 61 of the 1974 Act and comply with the detailed requirements of the Consumer Credit (Agreements) Regulations 1983 (SI 1983/1553). A consumer hire agreement is defined as "an agreement made by a person with an individual (the 'hirer') for the hiring of goods to the hirer, being an agreement which (a) is not a hire-purchase agreement, and (b) is capable of subsisting for more than three months". Provided the lessee is not a body corporate, there is no requirement that an individual lessee must be a "consumer". Hence, the lessee may indeed be a businessperson and the contract a commercial contract of hire. Moreover, where the contract of hire falls within the definition of a consumer hire agreement, the 1974 Act imposes various restrictions on the advertising and canvassing of such hirings by lessors. The lessee also enjoys the other protections contained in the 1974 Act, eg the restricted rights to cancel the agreement in ss 67–73.

UCTA controls

The contract of hire will also be regulated by the Unfair Contract Terms Act 1977 ("UCTA") insofar as the lessor or lessee purports to exclude or restrict liability in respect of a breach of the common law implied terms. Section 15(2)(a) of UCTA expressly provides so. Thus, clauses excluding liability for breach of duty in the course of a business arising from a common law implied term will be subject to the "fairness and reasonableness" test by virtue of s 16 of UCTA. Moreover, where the contract of hire falls within the definition of a "consumer contract" or amounts to a "standard form contract", s 17 of UCTA will apply. Therefore, the exclusion or restriction of liability for breach of a contractual obligation (on the part of the lessor or the lessee) in a contract of hire will be prevented unless it is fair and reasonable to do so. A "consumer contract" is defined in s 25(1) of UCTA and is a contract in which one party to the contract deals in the course of a business and the other party ("the consumer") does not and, in the case of a contract of hire, the goods are of a type ordinarily supplied for private use or consumption. It will usually be the lessee who argues that he is a consumer. Meanwhile, the meaning of "standard form contract" is not set out in UCTA.

Supply of Goods and Services Act 1982

Sections 11G–11L of the 1982 Act are the relevant sections which apply to contracts of hire and reflect the implied terms which apply to contracts for the sale of goods and contracts of hire-purchase. Section 11L of the 1982 Act stipulates that where the 1982 Act is applicable and it is not excluded in the contract of hire, the *G M Shepherd* case does not apply and the common law implied terms are supplemented but are not overridden or repealed.

Lessor's right to transfer possession

Section 11H of the 1982 Act provides that there is an implied term which gives the lessor the right to transfer possession of the goods to the lessee by way of hire for the period of the hire.

Lessee's right to enjoy quiet possession

Secondly, the lessee is entitled to enjoy quiet possession of the goods for the period of hire. However, there is an exception so that possession may be disturbed by the owner (eg where the contract of hire between the lessor and lessee is a sub-lease and the lessor is not the owner of the goods) or some other person entitled to the benefit of any charge or encumbrance disclosed or known to the lessee before the contract is made.

Lessor's duty to ensure goods correspond to description

Where the lessee hires goods from the lessor by description, s 11I of the 1982 Act stipulates that there is an implied term that the goods will correspond to the description. Section 11I(4) of the 1982 Act directs that a contract may amount to a contract of hire of goods corresponding to description where the goods are selected by the lessee.

Lessor's duty to ensure goods correspond to sample

Section 11K states that where the lessor hires or agrees to hire the goods by reference to a sample, there is an implied term that (1) the bulk will correspond with the sample in quality, (2) the lessee will have a reasonable opportunity of comparing the bulk with the sample and (3) the goods will be free from any defect, making their quality unsatisfactory, which would not be apparent on reasonable examination of the sample.

Lessor's satisfactory quality duty

Section 11J of the 1982 Act deals with the quality and fitness for purpose of the goods hired to the lessee. It is stipulated that where goods are supplied by the lessor to the lessee in the course of the lessor's business, there is an implied term that the goods supplied under that contract are of satisfactory quality. Thus, private hires are excluded. The test for determining whether goods are of satisfactory quality is specified in s 11J(3) of the 1982 Act. It is provided that goods are deemed to be of satisfactory quality where they meet the standard that a reasonable person would regard as satisfactory, taking account of any description of the goods, the consideration for the hire (if relevant) and all the other relevant circumstances. However, where the contract of hire is a "consumer contract", in determining whether the goods are of a satisfactory quality, consideration must also be given to any public statements made by the hirer, producer or his representative about the specific characteristics of the goods, particularly in advertising or on labelling.

Lessor's fitness for purpose duty

Section 11J(5) and (6) of the 1982 Act set out the fitness for purpose implied term. Thus, where the lessor hires goods in the course of a business to the lessee and the lessee, expressly or by implication, makes known to the lessor in the course of negotiations conducted by him in relation to the making of the contract any particular purpose for which the goods are being hired, there is an implied term that the goods supplied under the contract are reasonably fit for that purpose, whether or not that is a purpose for which such goods are commonly supplied. However, the fitness for purpose implied term is inapplicable where the lessee does not rely, or it is unreasonable for him to rely, on the skill or judgement of the lessor.

Disapplication of statutory implied terms

Section 11L of the 1982 Act stipulates that where a right, duty or liability would arise under an implied term of the contract of hire, it may be excluded or varied by the parties by express agreement or by a course of dealing between them, or by such usage as binds both parties to the contract of hire. An express term is deemed to exclude or vary an implied term where it is deemed to be inconsistent with that implied term. Needless to say, these provisions which permit the contracting out of implied terms are subject to the statutory constraints on exclusion and limitation of liability clauses contained in UCTA and so may be susceptible to review in terms of the "fair and reasonable" test contained therein.

Essential Facts

- There are four modern forms of the contract of hire, namely the finance lease, the operating lease, the contract hire and the rental or hire agreement.
- There are four essential elements to the contract of hire, namely a thing to be let, a passing rent, the consent of the contracting parties and a specified period of let.

- The common law and the Supply of Goods and Services Act 1982 impose various implied terms into the contract of hire.
- Those implied terms impose obligations on the lessor and the lessee.

Essential Cases

Wilson v Orr (1879): although the passing rent should be in money, rather than money's worth, the Court of Session was prepared to classify the hire of a horse in return for a rent comprised of providing the horse's keep as a contract of hire.

Wilson v Norris (1810): there is a common law implied term that the lessor is under a duty to deliver the subjects of hire to the lessee in a state of good condition and repair.

G M Shepherd Ltd v North West Securities Ltd (1991): in the case of a finance lease or operating lease where the lessor is not involved in the selection of the hired goods, the contract will be treated as a *sui generis* contract (ie not as a contract of hire) and so the implied term that the lessor has a good unencumbered title to the goods will not apply.

Seton v Paterson (1880): where a horse was hired for the purpose of undertaking a day's journey, but was taken for a gallop race by the lessee, the lessee was held to be in breach of the implied term to use the horse for the purpose for which it was let.

Campbell v Lord Kennedy (1828): the lessee of a horse was deemed to be in breach of the implied term to take proper care of the goods hired where he lent the horse to a friend whose actions resulted in the horse catching a chill and dying.

3 AGENCY

Businesses often engage agents to act on their behalf as intermediaries to sell their products or services. The reasons for engaging an agent range from lack of time, lack of expertise to lack of knowledge of a particular marketplace. The law of agency regulates the relationship amongst a principal, an agent and a third party. The principal is the person on whose behalf the agent acts, the agent is the party who has power to act as an intermediary on behalf of the principal and the third party is the party who enters into a contract with the principal through the agent.

In this chapter, the law of agency will be analysed in detail. First, the different types of agency and the constitution of the agency relationship will be considered. Secondly, the nature of an agent's authority to bind the principal in contract or otherwise and the rights and obligations of each of the parties to the agency relationship will be explored. Finally, consideration will be given to the termination of the agency relationship and the implications of termination.

SOURCES OF AGENCY LAW

The common law is the main source of the law of agency. However, the Commercial Agents (Council Directive) Regulations 1993 (SI 1993/3053) ("the Regulations") contain a number of special rules which apply to some agency relationships.

DEFINITION OF AGENT AND TYPES OF AGENT

No strict legal definition of an agent has been approved by the courts in Scotland. Professor Sir T B Smith submitted the following definition of agency, which, whilst useful, is technically not wholly comprehensive:

> "a person who has authority to act for and on behalf of another (called the principal) in contracting legal relations with third parties; and the agent representing the principal creates, alters, or discharges legal obligations of a contractual nature between the latter and third parties".

Thus, the agency relationship is tripartite, envisaging a principal, an agent and a third party. The agent will be paid a fee in respect of his expertise in the local market over which he has been appointed and will usually have the power to bind the principal contractually with third parties. However, as stated, the above definition is under-inclusive. For example, the Regulations provide their own definition of a commercial agent which is distinct from the above definition. Regulation 2(1) of the Regulations provides that a commercial agent is a self-employed intermediary who has continuing authority to negotiate the sale or purchase of goods on behalf of his principal, or to negotiate and conclude the sale or purchase of goods on behalf of and in the name of that principal.

General and special agents

Agents may be classified into distinct groupings which highlight the nature of the (implied) authority to bind the principal which they enjoy and also commonly serve to outline the nature of the agent's relationship with the principal or third parties. For example, a general agent is understood to be an agent who is engaged to carry out any or all of the business of a principal. Whilst the matter is not free from doubt (see Bell's *Principles*, s 219(7)), it appears to be the case that a solicitor will be a general agent. Meanwhile, a special agent is an agent who is authorised to carry out one specific particular transaction or a series of identifiable transactions (eg *Morrison* v *Statter* (1885)).

CONSTITUTION OF AGENCY

An agency relationship does not require to be created in writing and an oral agency is valid. However, where the relationship between an agent and a principal is one of commercial agency in terms of reg 2(1) of the Regulations, reg 13 of the Regulations confers upon a party the right to call on the other to produce a written signed document setting out the terms of the agency contract including any terms subsequently agreed. An agency may be created by conduct where the agent commences acting on behalf of a principal. The effect of that rule is that the agency relationship may be constituted expressly (ie in writing or orally) or impliedly (ie by conduct). Another form of agency, known as *negotiorum gestio*, arises by operation of law where the administration of the affairs of a mentally incapable person is conducted of necessity by a person who is deemed to be an agent. Here, there is no requirement for offer and acceptance and the agency relationship is created by necessity. Finally, an agency relationship may be constituted in the absence of offer and acceptance by ratification by the principal. Such ratification will be relevant where a person, without the prior authority of the principal, purports to bind the principal in contract with a third party and the principal elects to retrospectively ratify the actions of that person.

THE AGENT'S AUTHORITY

Express and implied authority

An agent's authority may be express, implied or ostensible/apparent. One of the objectives of the rules on authority is to protect third parties. Express authority arises where the principal has specifically given the agent authority to enter into particular transactions on its behalf or to engage in certain conduct on its behalf. Usually, such authority will be conferred in a written agreement entered into between the agent and the principal or orally. An agent may also have implied authority by virtue of the nature of his agency. For example, a general agent will have the authority to carry out any or all of the business of the principal. However, not so in the case of a special agent. Likewise, a mercantile agent in the context of the Factors Act 1889 will have implied authority to sell or buy the goods of the principal.

Ostensible/apparent authority

In the case of ostensible/apparent authority, an agent exceeds his authority. Nevertheless, provided certain criteria are satisfied, the third party with whom the agent has dealt will be protected from the unauthorised agent's actions and the principal will be bound by the contract concluded by the agent and liable to the third party on the contract. Where the doctrine of apparent/ostensible authority applies, the principal is precluded from denying the agent's authority to the third party or to act inconsistently so as to give the third party conflicting messages. For that reason, ostensible/apparent authority is an example of personal bar on the part of the principal.

Criteria for establishment of ostensible/apparent authority

The leading authority which defines the main criteria for the establishment of ostensible/apparent authority is the English case of *Freeman & Lockyer* v *Buckhurst Park Properties (Mangal) Ltd* (1964) which was approved by Lord President Hope in the Inner House of the Court of Session in *Dornier GmbH* v *Cannon* (1991). Thus, ostensible/apparent authority necessitates the existence of each of the following elements:

- a legal relationship between the principal and the third party contractor created by a representation made by the principal to the third party contractor;
- that representation must have been intended to be and in fact must have been acted on by the third party contractor;
- that representation must have been to the effect that the agent has the authority to enter on behalf of the principal into a contract of a kind within the scope of the agent's apparent authority in such terms to render the principal liable to perform any obligations imposed on him by such a contract.

Key criteria

With regard to the first criterion, it is crucial that the principal represents to the third party that the agent does not lack authority. This may be in writing, orally or by positive or negative conduct, ie the principal's actions or omissions (*Freeman & Lockyer* v *Buckhurst Park Properties (Mangal) Ltd* (1964)). The third party must also demonstrate that it relied on the principal's representation and that loss was sustained as a result of such reliance. Moreover, the third party is under an obligation to show that the conduct of the principal caused it to believe that the agent had authority to enter into the contract. The result of the latter rule is that if the third party has knowledge from another source that the agent is exceeding his authority, it will be impossible for the third party to establish a causal link between the principal's actions or omissions and the third party's "belief" that the agent has authorisation. Accordingly, the third party will be unable to obtain the benefit of the doctrine of ostensible/apparent authority (*Colvin* v *Dixon* (1867)).

Alternative means for the creation of ostensible authority

Ostensible/apparent authority may be created through a course of dealing. For example, where an agent at one point had general authority to carry out all of the business of the principal (and so is a general agent), but the principal then terminates the agent's general authority without notifying third party contractors, ostensible/apparent authority may arise in respect of a third party who deals regularly with that agent. Of course, if the third party becomes aware through one source or another that the agent's authority has come to an end, that third party will be precluded from relying on the doctrine of ostensible/apparent authority (*North of Scotland Banking Corp* v *Behn, Moller & Co* (1881)). The counsel of perfection is for the principal to make it clear to third party customers that the authority of the agent has ceased either through correspondence or general advertisements. A good example of that process is set out in the case of partners as agents in s 36 of the Partnership Act 1890.

Effect of ostensible authority

In circumstances where the third party is able to establish each of these criteria, it is important to stress that the effect of the establishment of ostensible/apparent authority is not to validate the contract or to cure the agent's lack of authority. The contract remains invalid and the agent remains unauthorised. However, the effect is that the principal is personally barred from claiming that the agent lacked authority in any action raised by the third party against the principal based on the contract, eg an action for the recovery of damages for the loss sustained by the third party in respect of a breach of the principal's obligations under the contract.

Ratification

Where the agent has exceeded his authority and none of the rules on express, implied or ostensible/apparent authority operates to cure the position, then if the agent has purported to bind the principal in contract, the general rule is that the principal will not be bound. However, provided certain criteria are fulfilled, the principal may unilaterally ratify (expressly, impliedly or from its actions or omissions) the agent's conduct. The principal's ratification may relate to either an existing agent's lack of authority or a person who is not actually an agent of the principal. In this latter scenario the ratifying conduct of the principal operates to create an agency relationship where none had existed before (*Alexander Ward & Co Ltd* v *Samyang Navigation Co Ltd* (1975)). Ratification functions in a retrospective manner whereby a contractual relationship is deemed to have existed between the principal and a third party contractor from the moment that the agent purported to bind the principal.

Criteria for ratification

There are certain prerequisites which must be satisfied for valid ratification to operate. First, there must be a principal in existence at the point at which the agent (who lacks the necessary authority) purports to bind the principal in contract with a third party. If the principal did not exist at that point in time, the principal has no power to ratify and so the agent may find themselves personally liable on the contract with the third party. This criterion is particularly important where the principal is a body corporate and is not incorporated when the agent seeks to bind it in contract with the third party (see s 51(1) of the Companies Act 2006). Secondly, if the principal does exist at that time, it must also have legal capacity at that time and also when it purports to ratify the agent's actions (*Boston Deep Sea Fishing and Ice Co Ltd v Farnham* (1957)). Thus, if the contract between the principal and the third party is beyond the statutory powers of the principal, ie *ultra vires* (eg in the case of a public body), ratification will be impossible. Thirdly, the contract must not be void or illegal. Fourthly, if it is alleged that the principal unilaterally ratified the agent's actions by its actions or omissions, there must be evidence to enable an inference to be drawn that the principal was fully briefed of all relevant facts. Thus, if there is some gap or error in the principal's knowledge regarding the actions of the agent, there will be evidence that the principal was not fully aware of all relevant facts and that its purported ratification was defective. Fifthly, there must be evidence to demonstrate that the agent entered into the transaction with the third party as an agent. For example, in circumstances where a person enters into a contract with a third party on their own account, there would be insufficient evidence to enable a principal to ratify the actions of that person to create an agency relationship afresh. The rationale for that rule is that the "agent" did not actually enter into the agreement with the third party on behalf of the principal, but instead for his own personal purposes. Thus, ratification is precluded (*Keighley, Maxsted & Co v Durant* (1901)). Sixthly, there is a rule to the effect that the principal must ratify within a specified time limit where the actions of the agent which require to be ratified are subject to such a time limit (*Goodall v Bilsland* (1909)). Finally, whilst the position is not wholly clear in Scots law, there may be a rule which mirrors English law to the effect that ratification will be precluded where it results in prejudice to the interests of third parties. For example, where a principal ratifies, the third party's power to withdraw from the contract will terminate. In certain circumstances, the effect of the ratification may be detrimental to the interests of the third party and Scots law may indeed develop a rule which deprives such ratification of legal validity.

THE DUTIES OF THE AGENT AND THE RIGHTS OF THE PRINCIPAL

Duties of the agent

The agent's duties may be divided into non-fiduciary duties and fiduciary duties. The first non-fiduciary duty imposes an obligation on the agent to follow the principal's instructions. If the principal's instructions are unclear, the agent is not liable. Regulation 3(2)(c) of the Regulations imposes an obligation on a commercial agent to comply with reasonable instructions given by the principal. In terms of *Gilmour* v *Clark* (1853), if the agent breaches the instructions of the principal, he is liable in damages for any loss suffered by the principal. Secondly, the agent must exercise skill and care in performing his obligations. The standard of care is based on a mixture of an objective and subjective test. Thus, if the agent is a qualified chartered accountant, his subjective qualities and skills will operate to lift the objective standard of care so that his duty will be that of a reasonably competent and careful member of the accountancy profession. Where the agent fails to meet the relevant standard of care and so breaches his duty, he will be liable to the principal in damages. The final non-fiduciary duty of the agent is to keep accounts in writing or in some other more informal medium, depending on what has been agreed between the agent and the principal.

Introduction to fiduciary duties

The law recognises that the relationship between the agent and the principal is one of mutual trust and good faith. Thus, the principal duty is for the agent to act in good faith and disclose all facts and circumstances with regard to the principal's business (Bell's *Principles*, s 222). Regulation 3(1) of the Regulations builds on the common law duty of good faith by providing that all commercial agents must look after the interests of their principals and act dutifully and in good faith. In terms of reg 3(2) of the Regulations, this includes the agent (1) making proper efforts to negotiate and, where appropriate, concluding the transactions he is instructed to take care of, (2) communicating to the principal all the necessary information available to him and (3) complying with reasonable instructions given by the principal.

The fiduciary duties

The first fiduciary duty to consider is the agent's duty to account to the principal in respect of all benefits received in connection with the principal's business. Sums generated in the course of the agency business must be accounted for, eg commissions and other sums in money or money's worth. However, in terms of *Lothian* v *Jenolite Ltd* (1969), an agent does not require to account for extra income he has generated by working for a competitor of the principal in the absence of a non-competition restrictive covenant. Where the agent breaches this fiduciary duty, the remedy is an action of accounting rather than damages, ie the gain enjoyed by the agent may be disgorged and transferred to the principal. However, if the agent has not enjoyed any gain, the principal's action will be incompetent (*Sao Paolo Alpargatas SA* v *Standard Chartered Bank Ltd* (1985)).

Secondly, there is a fiduciary duty to the effect that the agent must not disclose or exploit confidential information regarding the business of the principal. Thirdly, a duty is imposed to the effect that the agent is disentitled from entering into transactions whereby the agent generates a profit at the principal's expense – the so-called "no-profit" rule (*Cunningham* v *Lee* (1874)). Fourthly, the agent may delegate his duties to a third party subject to certain exceptions. Those exceptions reflect the fact that the agent has been specifically chosen to perform by the principal, ie *delectus personae* applies. Finally, there is a duty to relieve the principal of any liability suffered as a result of the agent entering into any contract in excess of authority – see *Milne* v *Ritchie* (1882).

THE DUTIES OF THE PRINCIPAL AND THE RIGHTS OF THE AGENT

Principal's duties

Where the agency is a commercial agency, reg 4(1) of the Regulations stipulates that the principal must act dutifully and in good faith towards the commercial agent. In particular, the principal must provide the commercial agent with the necessary documentation relating to the goods concerned and obtain for the commercial agent the information necessary for the performance of the agency contract, and in particular notify the agent within a reasonable period once he anticipates that the volume of commercial transactions will be significantly lower than that which the commercial agent could normally have expected. Moreover, the principal is under an obligation to inform the agent within a reasonable period of his acceptance or refusal of, and of any non-execution by him of, a commercial transaction which the commercial agent has procured for him.

The agent's rights: payment

Mackersy's Executors v *St Giles Cathedral Managing Board* (1904) directs that there is a presumption that the agent is entitled to be paid for services rendered where the agency represents his livelihood. Of course, usually an express term is included in a written agency agreement setting out the remuneration of the agent, including whether he is to be paid a flat fee or commission on sales generated. The common law provides that commission will be payable in the event that the transaction was concluded as a result of the actings of the agent or the agent's actions materially contributed to the same (*Walker, Fraser & Steele v Fraser's Trustees* (1910)). Where the agent is a commercial agent and the agreement entered into between the agent and the principal does not stipulate the agent's payment terms, reg 6 of the Regulations assumes importance. Here, it is provided that the commercial agent is entitled to the remuneration that commercial agents appointed for the goods forming the subject of the agency contract are customarily allowed in the place where the agent carries on his activities. If there is no such customary practice, a commercial agent is entitled to reasonable remuneration taking into account all the aspects of the transaction. Regulations 7 and 8 also provide for the payment of commission to the commercial agent on commercial transactions during the period covered by the agency contract and beyond.

The agent's rights: reimbursement of expenses and lien

The commercial agent has a right to be reimbursed in respect of all expenses incurred in the proper performance of his duties. This right is accompanied by a right of relief relative to all liabilities sustained by the agent in the proper performance of his duties. Finally, the agent enjoys a right of lien over the goods of the principal in security for payment of commission or other remuneration.

THIRD-PARTY CONTRACTS

Where third parties enter into contracts with the principal through the intervention of the agent, the general rule is that the agent does not become contractually bound to the third party despite the fact that he has undertaken the work in ensuring the conclusion of such a contract. Where an agent discloses that he is an agent, the effect on contractual relations between the principal and the third party depends on the nature of the agent's communication with the third party regarding the existence and identity of the principal. The legal position is best analysed by categorising circumstances into three elements:

(1) where the agent discloses that he is an agent, that there is a principal and identifies the principal;

(2) where the agent discloses that he is an agent, that there is a principal but fails to name and identify the principal; and

(3) where the agent fails to inform the third party that there was a principal on whose behalf he was acting.

Scenario 1

Here, the principal will be bound into a contract with the third party and the agent will incur no personal liability (*Stone and Rolfe Ltd* v *Kimber Coal Co Ltd* (1926)). *Armour* v *T L Duff & Co* (1912) ruled that the position will be the same where the principal is not specifically named but the principal can be identified with little effort. However, in certain contexts it is either customary or standard practice for agents to specifically incur personal liability on a contract entered into between the principal and the third party, eg when solicitors enter into letters of obligation in respect of transactions involving the conveyance of heritage by their clients.

Scenario 2

Here, the Scots law position is not particularly clear. In certain circumstances, it will be possible for the court to identify the principal and, here, the agent will bear no personal liability. However, where it is not possible to ascertain the name of the principal from the surrounding circumstances, then the third party has a choice; the third party may elect to hold the principal or the agent personally liable on the contract in terms of the cases of *Lamont Nisbett & Co* v *Hamilton* (1907) and *Ferrier* v *Dods* (1865). However, if the agent declines to name the principal when asked to do so, the agent will incur personal liability (*Gibb* v *Cunningham and Robertson* (1925)).

Scenario 3

Where the agent fails to disclose the existence of a principal, the general rule is that the agent incurs liability to the third party with whom he contracts unless the third party, on learning of the existence of the principal, elects to hold the principal liable. Moreover, an agent for an undisclosed principal will be personally liable in damages for personal injuries sustained by a third party where the latter is working on the premises of the undisclosed principal (*Ruddy* v *Monte Marco* (2008)). However, the liability is not alternative, ie the third party cannot choose to sue both the principal and agent and must hold one liable or the other (*Bennett* v *Inveresk Paper Co* (1891)). However, there are circumstances where a written contract is concluded between the agent and the third party and it is impossible as a matter of implication or interpretation for the third party to elect to hold that the principal is liable.

Ratification in context of undisclosed principal

In circumstances where a principal fails to ratify the actions of an agent who has exceeded his authority, the agent may or may not be personally liable on the contract with the third party. Bell, *Commentaries*, I, 543 directs that it is not always the case that the agent will be personally bound and in circumstances where the agent is not so personally liable to the third party, it may be the case that no contract subsists between the agent and the third party at all. Whatever the position, what is certain is that no contract will arise between the principal and the third party. The third party will be left with an option to sue the principal based on breach of apparent authority or the agent on the basis of breach of warranty of authority.

TERMINATION OF THE AGENCY CONTRACT

Common law termination

A distinction requires to be made between termination of the agency contract at common law and termination of a commercial agency contract. First, with regard to common law termination, it is recognised that the agency contract may be determined by the expiry of a fixed-term contract, by mutual agreement or in circumstances where the objective of the agency relationship has ended (*Rhodes* v *Forwood* (1875)). It is also understood that the principal or agent may unilaterally revoke the agency relationship unless there is an express term to the contrary in the agency contract. Where one of the parties elects unilaterally to revoke, Erskine, *Institute*, III, 3, 40 stipulates that that person may be liable in damages in respect of losses incurred by the other party as a result of early termination (*Turner* v *Goldsmith* (1891)). The mental incapacity of the agent will put an end to the agent's authority (*Drew* v *Nunn* (1878)). Finally, since the law treats the agency relationship as one involving *delectus personae*, the death of the agent or principal automatically terminates the agency contract.

Termination of commercial agency: notice periods

In the case of a commercial agency, the provisions concerning the periods of notice of termination in the Regulations will demand consideration. It is provided in reg 15(2)(a), (b) and (c) of the Regulations that either party seeking to terminate the agency contract must give a minimum of 1 month's notice to the other in the first year of the agency contract, 2 month's notice to the other in the second year and 3 months' where the contract has endured for 3 years or more. Since these are minimum periods of notice, it is possible for the agency contract to stipulate longer periods.

Termination of commercial agency: payment of compensation or indemnity

On termination, an agent has the right to be paid compensation or indemnity. Regulation 19 of the Regulations directs that any provision of an agency contract which purports to exclude the agent's right to be paid compensation or indemnity is void. In the absence of provision in the agency contract stipulating for indemnity, reg 17(2) of the Regulations states that the commercial agent is entitled to compensation. Regulation 17(9) narrates that if the commercial agent fails to notify the principal within 1 year following the termination of the agency contract that he intends to pursue his entitlement for compensation or indemnity, then his claim becomes time-barred. Regulation 18 goes on to list a series of situations where the agent's right to be paid compensation or indemnity on termination is expressly excluded: first, where the principal terminates the agency contract due to a breach or default which has been caused by frustration of the agency contract; and, secondly where the agent has terminated the agency contract. However, there are exceptions to this general rule: first, where the agent's actions in terminating the agency contract are attributable to the principal's breach of contract; and, secondly, the agent has a right to be paid compensation or indemnity where he was justified in terminating the agency contract on the grounds of age, infirmity or serious illness.

Indemnity

From a principal's perspective, it will usually be the case that the payment of an indemnity is preferable over the payment of compensation, since the sums payable to the agent in terms of an indemnity are capped at 1 year's commission duly calculated on the basis of the average of the last 5 years of the agency or, if the agency has endured for a shorter period, the annual average over the period of the agency. This can be contrasted with the sums payable to the agent in terms of compensation, which are open-ended. The purpose of the indemnity payment is to enable the agent to gain some advantage from the increase in the principal's business which has been generated as a result of his activities (reg 17(3)). The grant of an indemnity does not preclude the agent from seeking damages.

Compensation

Regulation 17(6) of the Regulations specifically provides that the objective of compensation is to compensate the agent for the damage suffered as a result of the premature termination of the agency relationship. Regulation 17(7) sets out further details of how such damage is calculated to the effect that it is deemed to occur particularly when the termination takes place in either or both of the following circumstances, namely circumstances which (a) deprive the commercial agent of the commission which proper performance of the agency contract would have procured for him whilst providing his principal with substantial benefits linked to the activities of the commercial agent, or (b) have not enabled the commercial agent to amortise the costs and expenses that he had incurred in the performance of the agency contract on the advice of his principal.

The approach of the courts towards the calculation of compensation was dealt with by the Scottish courts in *King* v *T Tunnock Ltd* (2000) and by the House of Lords on an appeal from an English case in *Lonsdale* v *Howard & Hallam Ltd* (2007). In *King*, it was held that the mode of calculation of compensation deployed by French law which awards 2 years' loss of average gross commission ought to be applied. Mr King had been engaged as a commercial agent for Tunnocks for approximately 32 years when his agency contract was terminated. On the basis of the lengthy duration of the agency relationship, the Court of Session valued his commission in accordance with the French model, namely 2 years' loss of average gross commission. However, in *Lonsdale*, Lord Hoffmann in the House of Lords declined to follow the French model of awarding 2 years' loss of average gross commission and ruled that the courts enjoy discretion in fixing the level of compensation. Lord Hoffmann took the view that this approach would be fortified in a case such as *Lonsdale*, where the business of the principal was in prolonged decline. His Lordship was of the view that the better way of analysing the calculation of compensation was to understand that the agent was being compelled to hand back the goodwill of the principal's business which the agent had been involved in creating at the point of termination.

Essential Facts

- The Scots law of agency is regulated by the common law and the Commercial Agents (Council Directive) Regulations 1993.
- The law of agency regulates the relationship which arises amongst a principal, an agent and a third party.
- The principal is the person on whose behalf the agent acts, the agent is the party who has power to act as an intermediary on behalf of the principal and the third party is the party who enters into a contract with the principal through the agent.
- Agents may be special or general, which is descriptive of the authority which that agent wields.
- An agency relationship does not require to be created in writing and an oral agency is valid.
- An agent's authority may be express, implied or ostensible/apparent.
- Express authority arises where the principal has specifically given the agent authority to enter into particular transactions on its behalf or to engage in certain conduct on its behalf.
- An agent may have implied authority by virtue of the nature of the agency, eg a general agent will have the authority to carry out any or all of the business of the principal.
- Ostensible/apparent authority arises where a representation is made by the principal to a third party that the agent has the authority to enter on behalf of the principal into a contract of a kind within the scope of the agent's authority.
- Where an agent exceeds his authority, in certain circumstances, the principal may ratify the agent's conduct.
- The agent's duties may be divided into fiduciary and non-fiduciary duties.
- The agent has a right to be remunerated, a right to recover expenses, a right of lien and, in the case of a commercial agency, the principal must act dutifully and in good faith towards the commercial agent.
- The extent of an agent's liability to a third party on a contract depends on whether the agent (1) discloses that he is an agent, (2) discloses that there is a principal and/or (3) identifies a principal.

- At common law, the agency contract may be determined by the expiry of a fixed-term contract, by mutual agreement or in circumstances where the objective of the agency relationship has ended. The principal or agent may unilaterally revoke the agency relationship unless there is an express term to the contrary in the agency contract; and the death of the agent or principal automatically terminates the agency contract.
- Where a commercial agency is terminated by the principal, the agent will be entitled to be paid compensation or an indemnity.

Essential Cases

Morrison v Statter (1885): distinguishes a special agent from a general agent.

Freeman & Lockyer v Buckhurst Park Properties (Mangal) Ltd (1964): articulates the three elements for the establishment of ostensible/apparent authority.

Keighley, Maxsted & Co v Durant (1901): one of the prerequisites of ratification is that the agent must have entered into the transaction with the third party as an agent.

Gilmour v Clark (1853): if the agent breaches the principal's instructions, he is liable in damages for any loss suffered by the principal.

Cunningham v Lee (1874): the agent is under a fiduciary duty not to enter into transactions whereby the agent generates a profit at the principal's expense – the so-called "no-profit" rule.

Milne v Ritchie (1882): an agent is under a fiduciary duty to relieve the principal of any liability suffered as a result of the agent entering into any contract in excess of authority.

Mackersy's Executors v St Giles Cathedral Managing Board (1904): there is a common law presumption that the agent is entitled to be paid for services rendered where the agency represents his livelihood.

Walker, Fraser & Steele v Fraser's Trustees (1910): the common law provides that commission will be payable to the agent where a transaction was concluded as a result of the actings of the agent or the agent's actions materially contributed to the same.

Lonsdale v Howard & Hallam Ltd (2007): on the termination of a commercial agency, the agent should be compensated in respect of the goodwill of the principal's business which he is being asked to hand back to the principal at the point of termination and for which he had been actively involved in creating during the subsistence of the agency relationship.

4 INSURANCE

Insurance is an incredibly important commercial activity in the UK. Since the inception of the insurance market, the law has recognised the need to regulate this sphere of commercial activity. The law achieves this through a mixture of common law and statutory regulation.

PURPOSE OF INSURANCE

As expressed in the introduction, the objective of an insured in entering into an insurance contract is to protect himself against the occurrence of a particular misfortune or particular risks: eg motor insurance protects the insured in the event that his vehicle is damaged or destroyed. The nature of that protection (ie whether the insured has a right of repair or a right to be paid compensation for loss) is regulated by the terms of the insurance contract. However, the crucial point is that in some way the insured will be safeguarded in the event that the perils or risks described in the insurance contract occur.

THE NATURE OF INSURANCE

There are essentially two types of insurance: first, there is indemnity insurance, which entitles the insured to indemnification from the insurer on the occurrence of an event or peril specified in the insurance contract, eg theft of property, fire insurance, building and contents insurance, etc. The second form of insurance is life assurance. In the case of indemnity assurance, the peril is uncertain to occur whereas, in the case of life assurance, it is certain that the life assured will come to an end at some point in time.

DEFINITION OF INSURANCE

There have been many attempts by the courts in Scotland and England to define an insurance contract. None have been completely satisfactory. The nearest approximation to a definition is contained in the case of *Prudential Insurance Co* v *Inland Revenue Commissioners* (1904). In terms of the *Prudential* definition, there are four elements which must be satisfied as follows:

(1) consideration must pass from the insured to the insurer (which is a periodical payment called the premium);

(2) the insured must secure a benefit, usually the payment of a sum of money;

(3) upon the happening of some event;

(4) which involves an element of uncertainty as to (a) whether the event will happen or not, or (b) the time at which it will happen.

Furthermore, the event referred to in (3) must be adverse to the interests of the insured (*Department of Trade and Industry* v *St Christopher's Motorists Association* (1974)).

CONSTITUTION OF CONTRACT OF INSURANCE

An insurance contract does not require to be reduced to writing in order to be legally valid in terms of Scots law. Section 1(1) of the Requirements of Writing (Scotland) Act 1995 stipulates that writing is not required for the constitution of any contract, including an insurance contract. However, in the context of marine insurance, s 22 of the Marine Insurance Act 1906 provides that a marine policy will not be admissible in court unless it is embodied in written form.

INSURABLE INTEREST

A party to an insurance contract must have insurable interest in the subject matter of insurance. In examining the nature of the interest which the insured must possess, it is beneficial to make a distinction between life assurance and indemnity insurance policies.

Life assurance

First, in the context of life assurance, s 1 of the Life Assurance Act 1774 states that an insurance policy will be void where a person takes out a life assurance policy over the life of another person in which he has no interest. The nature of that interest is stipulated in s 3 of the Life Assurance Act 1774. Here, the fundamental point is made that the interest must be of a pecuniary or financial variety. For example, a son will have insurable interest in the life of his father due to the son's financial right to the payment of aliment. Likewise, s 1 of the Married Women's Policies of Assurance (Scotland) Act 1880 narrates that a wife has the right to effect a policy of assurance on the life of her husband. In the case of *Dalby* v *India and London Life Assurance Co* (1854), it was ruled by the court that it was sufficient that the insured possessed an insurable interest in the life assured at the date the policy of insurance was effected. It is worthwhile stressing that an insurable interest of a pecuniary or financial interest is not necessarily limited to familial relationships. For example, in the case of *Turnbull & Co* v *Scottish Provident Institution* (1896), it was ruled by the Outer House of the Court of Session that a firm had a direct financial interest, and thus an insurable interest, in the life of its local agent in Iceland.

Indemnity insurance

Secondly, for the purposes of indemnity insurance, the nature of the insurable interest required was outlined in the landmark case of *Macaura* v *Northern Assurance Co Ltd* (1925). In *Macaura*, the insured was a creditor and sole shareholder of a limited company. The company owned a quantity of timber, much of which was stored on the land of the insured. The timber was insured in the name of the insured, not the name of the company. When the timber was destroyed by fire, the insured made a claim and the insurer resisted liability. The court ruled that the insured had no insurable interest in the timber. Only the company had an insurable interest. The court made the point that it is crucial that the insured has a legal or equitable interest in the property insured. Otherwise, the contract of insurance will be void for lack of insurable interest. Therefore, even in circumstances where an insured has an expectation of, or stands to sustain a loss as a result of, the destruction or damage of the subject matter of the insurance contract, this will be insufficient to entitle them to indemnification if they are unable to point to a legal or equitable interest.

Consequences of a lack of insurable interest

In the case of a life assurance policy, the consequences of a lack of insurable interest are clear: s 1 of the Life Assurance Act 1774 stipulates that the policy is "null and void". Meanwhile, in the case of indemnity insurance, the Scots common law provides that it is an essential element of a contract of insurance that there is a subject in which the insured has an interest (*The Laws of Scotland: Stair Memorial Encyclopaedia*, vol 12, para 848, citing Bell's *Principles*, s 457). Hence, without that essential element, the contract is void.

WARRANTIES

A warranty is a fundamental term of an insurance policy. It amounts to a promise made by the insured to the insurer. If the insured breaches the warranty then the rule in *Bank of Nova Scotia* v *Hellenic Mutual War Risk Association (Bermuda) Ltd ("The Good Luck")* (1992) will apply to the effect that the insurer is discharged from liability under the contract with effect from the date of the breach, ie the contract is not treated as void *ab initio*. It is irrelevant that there is no connection between the insured's breach and the insured's loss. For example, imagine the situation where an insured who has taken out a fire insurance policy suffers fire damage to cars stored on car dealership premises which he leases from a third-party landlord. If the insured has breached a warranty in the insurance policy to the effect that he operates a car dealership from property which he owns, the fact that there is no connection between the breach of that warranty and the financial loss occasioned to the insured as a result of the fire damage is irrelevant. Moreover, issues of materiality of breach are also irrelevant, since each breach of a warranty is treated as a material breach.

Types of warranty

In an insurance contract, there are essentially two types of warranty:

- a statement of fact by the insured as to the past or present (a "past/present fact warranty only"); or
- a continuing undertaking that a state of affairs will prevail throughout the duration of the policy, which must be exactly complied with, whether it be material to the risk insured or not (a "continuing/promissory warranty").

It is not always straightforward to ascertain whether a term of the policy amounts to a "past/present fact only warranty" or a "continuing/promissory warranty". It is often a matter of interpretation. For example, in the case of *Hussain* v *Brown* (1996), after some dispute between the insurer and the insured, the Court of Appeal ruled that the following words amounted to a "past/present fact only warranty": "Are the premises fitted with any system of intruder alarm. If yes give name of installing company."

For an example of a continuing warranty, see *Seavision Investments* v *Evennett and Clarkson Puckle ("The Tiburon")* (1992). In an insurance policy, a promissory warranty was granted by the insured to the effect that a vessel was and would be "of German flag, or ownership or management". In fact, the vessel was not of German flag, etc. As a result, when the ship was struck by an Exocet missile during the Iran/Iraq war, the breach of the warranty was held to be fatal to the claim since the insurer was automatically discharged from liability from the moment of the breach.

"Basis of the contract" clauses

How is it possible to tell whether a term of the policy is a past/present fact only warranty or a continuing/promissory warranty? No magic or special words are required, ie there is no need specifically to stipulate that the term is a warranty. Indeed, it is extremely common for insurance policies to provide that every term of the policy represents the "basis of the contract". Such a "basis of the contract" clause automatically elevates every term of the policy into a warranty (*Dawsons Ltd* v *Bonnin* (1922)).

A CONTRACT OF THE UTMOST GOOD FAITH

A contract of insurance is a contract "*uberrimae fidei*", ie one of the "utmost good faith" – *Carter* v *Boehm* (1766), *Stewart* v *Morison* (1779) and s 17 of the Marine Insurance Act 1906. However, unlike some other contracts which impose duties of good faith such as agency, the duty of good faith in the case of an insurance contract is imposed on the insured at particular times only, namely (i) immediately before the insurance contract is formed, ie at the negotiation stage and until the contract of insurance is formed and (ii) at the point of renewal of an insurance contract. As for the insurer, it is also under an obligation of good faith in certain circumstances to make disclosure to co-insureds, mortgagees/assignees or third party beneficiaries (*Bank of Nova Scotia* v *Hellenic Mutual War Risk Association (Bermuda) Ltd ("The Good Luck")* (1992) and *Banque Financière de la Cité SA* v *Westgate Insurance Co Ltd* (1991)).

The three elements of the "good faith" principle

The three components of the duty of good faith are as follows:

(1) duty of disclosure of all facts which are material to the risks insured in the insurance policy;

(2) duty not to misrepresent material facts; and

(3) duty not to make a fraudulent claim on the policy.

Each of the above will be considered in turn.

Duty of disclosure

There are two important issues to consider in the context of the duty of disclosure:

- the state of knowledge or belief of the insured about the relevance of certain facts to the risk insured; and
- the test of what is a "material" fact to the risks insured in terms of the insurance contract.

State of knowledge of the insured The first issue concerns the thorny problem of how the law treats the situation where the insured did not disclose a material fact but was unaware of that fact at the formation of the contract. In such a case, is the insurer relieved of liability to indemnify the insured in respect of any losses sustained? To answer this question, one must make a distinction between consumer insurance and commercial insurance. In the context of consumer insurance, the law asks, "Did the insured disclose what he knew or did he wilfully overlook/ turn a blind eye or conceal the factual position"? If he did not disclose what he did not know, the insurer is unable to avoid liability (see *Joel* v *Law Union & Crown Insurance* (1908) and *Economides* v *Commercial Union Assurance plc* (1998)). However, if he did not disclose what he knew and that factor would be material to the risk underwritten, the insurer would be entitled to negate liability. The difficulty arises where the insurer accepts that the insured was unaware of the relevant factor but asserts that the insured ought to have known about it but turned a blind eye to matters, ie that the insured had constructive knowledge. This issue was addressed in the cases of *Joel* v *Law Union & Crown Insurance* (1908) and *Economides* v *Commercial Union Assurance plc* (1998), where, in the context of consumer insurance, it was held that the insurer will be under a duty to indemnify the insured in circumstances where the insured did not know of the material fact and did not turn a wilful blind eye to matters.

However, in the case of marine insurance or insurance which is of a commercial nature, the law is as set out in s 18(1) of the Marine Insurance Act 1906. Here, the question becomes, "Did the insured disclose what he knew or ought to have known?" Moreover, in terms of s 18(1), the insured is deemed to know every circumstance which, in the ordinary course of business, ought to be known to him.

Test of materiality With regard to the test of materiality in the context of indemnity insurance, there are two possible interpretations as to what is material:

- whether the undisclosed fact would have had a "decisive influence" on the prudent insurer; or
- whether the fact is one which would have had an "effect" on the insurer's mind.

The second formulation is easier for an insurer to satisfy and was approved by the House of Lords (by a majority) in the case of *Pan Atlantic* v *Pine Top Industries Co Ltd* (1995). As a result of that decision, there is no need for an insurer to prove that a prudent insurer would have acted differently had it known of the fact in question. Instead, the insurer requires to show only that it was one factor the prudent insurer would have taken into account in deciding whether (i) to enter into the insurance contract or (ii) to set the premium at the level it did.

However, the test of materiality in Scotland in the context of life assurance differs from that applied in the case of indemnity insurance. It is more favourable to the insured. In *Life Association* v *Foster* (1873), it was held that what is material is determined by reference to what a reasonable insured would consider material, not what the prudent insurer would consider material. Thus, the test of materiality in the case of life assurance in Scots law is easier for an insured to satisfy.

Inducement In *Pan Atlantic* v *Pine Top Industries Co Ltd* (1995), it was ruled that the insurer must also prove inducement, ie that it was induced to enter into the contract or set the premium at the level it did as a result of the insured's non-disclosure.

Consequences of failure to disclose Where an insurer is able to demonstrate a failure on the part of the insured to disclose material factors and inducement, the insurer is entitled to reject liability. The insurance contract is treated as though it never existed, ie it is deemed to be void (see Marine Insurance Act 1906, s 17(1) and *Joel* v *Law Union & Crown Insurance Co* (1908). However, there is no right of damages. All sums paid out to the insured must be repaid and the premiums returned/refunded by the insurer to the insured.

Duty not to misrepresent material facts

An insured is under a duty not to misrepresent material facts. When expressing an opinion, an insured must not misrepresent matters. As regards the disclosure of representations of fact, the starting point is the statement in *Joel* v *Law Union & Crown Insurance Co* (1908) where it was stated that "the duty is a duty to disclose, and you cannot disclose what you do not know. The obligation to disclose, therefore, necessarily depends on the knowledge you possess". In expressing an opinion or making a representation of fact, the insured must act in good faith and honestly. In the context of consumer insurance, in the case of *Economides* v *Commercial Union Assurance plc* (1998), the Court of Appeal ruled that there is no requirement for the insured to show "reasonable grounds" for the belief which he holds in the relevant opinion expressed. The insured need demonstrate only that he had some basis for a belief which was genuinely held, not that the belief was reasonably justifiable. In other words, there is no duty on a consumer insured to enquire further into the facts than he did in order to discharge his obligation by having a "reasonable belief" in what he said. However, in the case of *M'Phee* v *Royal Insurance* (1979), it was suggested that in the context of commercial insurance, the insured must demonstrate that it had reasonable grounds for its belief.

Test of materiality, inducement and the consequences of misrepresentation As for the test of materiality, the position is exactly the same as the duty of disclosure, ie would the misrepresented fact have had an "effect" on the insurer's mind in underwriting the risk and setting the premium. Again, the onus is on the insurer to prove inducement, ie that had it known of the true position, it would have charged a higher premium or decided not to enter into the insurance policy. As with the duty of non-disclosure, the insurer is entitled to reject liability. However, there is no right of damages. All sums paid out to the insured must be repaid and the premiums returned/refunded by the insurer to the insured. However, if the misrepresentation is fraudulent as per the test in *Derry* v *Peek* (1889), then the insurer does not require to return the premiums paid to the insured.

Duty not to make a fraudulent claim

An insurer is under no liability to indemnify an insured where a fraudulent claim is made: *Black King Shipping Corporation* v *Massie ("The Litsion Pride")* (1985). If the insured makes a fraudulent claim or even a claim that is part genuine and part fraudulent, the insurer will be relieved of all further obligations under the contract. It is probable, but not actually settled by a court decision, that the insurer will have the option of avoiding the contract from its inception (which he would not normally want to do as that would involve him in having to return the premium).

EVENT INSURED

On grounds of public policy, the insurer will be entitled to avoid liability where it can demonstrate that the insured deliberately caused the loss suffered: *Beresford* v *Royal Insurance Company Ltd* (1938). Difficulties arise where the event insured is partly caused by the actions of the insured. In the case of *Dhak* v *Insurance Co of North America (UK) Ltd* (1996), an insured under a life assurance policy began abusing alcohol to relieve the pain caused by a back injury sustained at work. Tragically, she died 6 months later as a result of asphyxiation through intoxication. The insurer resisted liability on the ground of an exclusion in the life insurance policy in respect of death caused by deliberate means. The court held that the insurer was under no liability to pay out the insurance proceeds where the insured had deliberately engaged in the act of intoxicating herself and had taken a calculated risk. Of course, matters would have been different had the death been caused by accidental means.

Essential Facts

- An insurance contract protects an insured against the occurrence of a particular misfortune or particular risks.

- An insurance contract does not require to be reduced to writing in order to be legally valid in terms of Scots law: s 1(1) of the Requirements of Writing (Scotland) Act 1995.

- An insurance contract is a contract whereby for some consideration, usually but not necessarily for periodical payments called premiums, a person secures some benefit, usually but not necessarily the payment of a sum of money, upon the happening of some event, which event is adverse to the interests of that person and which involves an element of uncertainty as to (a) whether it will happen or not, or (b) the time at which it will happen.

- A party to an insurance contract must have insurable interest in the subject matter of insurance. Otherwise, the insurance contract is void.

- In the case of life assurance, the policy will be void where a person takes out a life assurance policy over the life of another person in which he has no pecuniary or financial interest.

- In the context of indemnity insurance, the insured must have a legal or equitable interest in the property insured.

- A warranty is a fundamental term of an insurance policy and, if breached, the insurer is discharged from liability under the contract with effect from the date of the breach.
- A contract of insurance is a contract "*uberrimae fidei*", ie one of the "utmost good faith".
- The duty of good faith can be divided into the insured's duty to disclose all facts which are material to the risks insured in the insurance policy, the insured's duty not to misrepresent material facts and the insured's duty not to make a fraudulent claim on the policy.

Essential Cases

Prudential Insurance Co v Inland Revenue Commissioners (1904): describes the four elements within the definition of the contract of insurance.

Dalby v India and London Life Assurance Co (1854): for the purposes of life assurance, the insured must possess an insurable interest in the life assured at the date the policy of insurance is effected.

Turnbull & Co v Scottish Provident Institution (1896): a firm had a direct financial interest, and thus an insurable interest, in the life of a local agent in Iceland.

Macaura v Northern Assurance Co Ltd (1925): a creditor, sole shareholder and director of a company did not have an insurable interest in respect of timber owned by the company and so the contract of insurance was invalid.

Bank of Nova Scotia v Hellenic Mutual War Risk Association (Bermuda) Ltd ("The Good Luck") (1992): on a breach of warranty by the insured, the insurer is discharged from liability under the contract with effect from the date of the breach.

Dawsons Ltd v Bonnin (1922): exemplifies the effect of a "basis of the contract" clause.

Carter v Boehm (1766), **Stewart v Morison (1779)**: a contract of insurance is a contract "*uberrimae fidei*".

Economides v Commercial Union Assurance plc (1998): in the context of consumer insurance, an insurer will be under a duty to indemnify the insured in such circumstances where the insured did not know of the material fact and did not turn a wilful blind eye to matters.

Pan Atlantic v Pine Top Industries Co Ltd (1995): in the context of indemnity insurance, a matter will be material if it would have had an effect on the mind of the insurer to write the premium or enter into the insurance contract.

Life Association v Foster (1873): in the case of life assurance, what is material is determined by reference to what a reasonable insured would consider material, not what the prudent insurer would consider material.

Black King Shipping Corporation v Massie ("The Litsion Pride") (1985): an insurer is under no liability to indemnify an insured where a fraudulent claim is made.

Beresford v Royal Insurance Company Ltd (1938): on grounds of public policy, the insurer will be entitled to avoid liability where it can be demonstrated that the insured deliberately caused the loss suffered.

5 RIGHTS IN SECURITY

When traders sell their goods or services to a purchaser, they may be paid money or money's worth on delivery or completion of performance. Alternatively, and much more commonly, the trader will supply on credit. However, with credit comes the risk that the trader ultimately may not be paid. For that reason, the trader will commonly call for security from the buyer or some other third party as protection. Likewise, where a lender extends a loan or other credit facilities to a borrower, in order to secure the repayment of the loan or credit plus interest and other costs, the lender will seek security from the borrower or a third party. The security obtained by the lender may be granted by the borrower or the third party and/or over the corporeal or incorporeal assets of the borrower or the third party.

PERSONAL RIGHTS IN SECURITY

Rights in security may be understood as personal or real rights and corresponding personal or real obligations. The difference between personal and real rights/obligations can be examined by first considering personal rights and obligations. Thus, where a trader or lender obtains a personal right to be paid the price for the goods sold or supplied from a third party or to have the loan repaid by a third party, that right translates into a corresponding obligation on the part of the third party to pay such price or repay such loan. Here, the obligation on the part of the third party is classified as a personal cautionary obligation or a personal guarantee and the trader or lender has a personal right to enforce that obligation against the third party cautioner. Thus, where the trader or lender is unable to obtain payment of the price for the goods sold or supplied or the repayment of the loan from the purchaser or the borrower, the former may enforce its personal cautionary rights to call on the third party to pay the balance of the price or the balance of the sum or loan remaining unpaid. Those rights and the corresponding obligations on the part of the third party are not real since they do not involve the trader or lender taking enforcement action over the assets and property of the third party. We will consider such personal cautionary obligations in detail in Chapter 6 on cautionary obligations.

REAL RIGHTS IN SECURITY

Personal cautionary obligations can be contrasted with real rights and obligations. Where a trader or lender obtains rights over the corporeal or incorporeal assets and property of the purchaser or borrower in security for the payment of the price for the goods sold or supplied or the repayment of the loan, those rights are categorised as real rights which translate into corresponding real obligations over the assets or property of the purchaser or borrower. The rights of the trader and lender are referred to as real rights and the obligations of the purchaser and borrower are classified as real obligations, since those rights and obligations subsist over the property of the latter. Thus, where the trader or lender is unable to obtain payment of the price for the goods sold or supplied or the repayment of the loan from the purchaser or the borrower, the former may enforce the real security which it has over the assets and property of the latter in order to recover the balance of the price or the loan remaining unpaid. We will examine such real rights in security and real obligations in greater detail in this chapter.

THE ACCESSORY NATURE OF RIGHTS IN SECURITY

In both the cases of personal cautionary obligations and real rights in security, the personal rights and obligations and real rights and obligations are accessory and collateral in nature. That is to say that they are (a) accessory to the primary right of the trader to be paid the price for the goods sold or supplied from the purchaser or for the lender to have the loan repaid from the borrower and (b) accessory to the corresponding primary obligation of the purchaser or the borrower to pay the trader the price for the goods sold or supplied or to repay the loan to the lender. Since these collateral personal rights and obligations and real rights and obligations are accessory or secondary in nature, they rely on the continuing existence of the primary right and corresponding primary obligation – when the primary right and obligation is extinguished, the general rule is that these accessory rights are also extinguished.

OUTLINE OF CHAPTER

In this chapter, we will explore *real rights in security* which may be sought and obtained by traders and lenders. The nature of the security depends on the underlying assets of the purchaser or borrower or third party which are secured, eg whether the assets are corporeal, incorporeal, heritable or moveable. In Chapter 6, we will subsequently move on to examine personal rights and obligations known as cautionary obligations. One of the legal considerations which distinguishes real rights in security from personal rights in security is that the latter do not require to be registered in a public register in order to be created whilst some of the former do indeed entail some form of registration or other public act to make them legally effective.

FIXED SECURITIES AND FLOATING SECURITIES

Fixed security

A distinction can be made between fixed and floating rights in security. A fixed security constitutes a real right in security in favour of a creditor or lender over an identified item of property. Since the property of the owner/debtor is the subject of a real right in security, the owner/debtor is disentitled from selling the assets in the ordinary course of business without first obtaining the consent of the creditor or lender. To that extent, the owner's power of disposal over the secured assets is circumscribed.

Floating security

A floating security does not confer a real right in security in favour of the creditor or lender. Instead, the security hovers over the assets and undertaking of the granter. It is only on the occurrence of specific events that the law provides that the floating security converts into a fixed security. Scots law recognises many forms of fixed security which are available over different kinds of property (eg corporeal moveables, incorporeal moveables, corporeal heritables, incorporeal heritables) whereas there is only one form of floating security recognised, namely the floating charge.

VOLUNTARY SECURITIES AND SECURITIES ARISING BY OPERATION OF LAW

Voluntary security

A real right in security can be created voluntarily by a debtor in favour of a creditor. Conversely, the security can arise automatically by operation of law. That is to say that securities arising by operation of law emerge without the agreement of the parties, ie involuntarily. The form of the voluntary real right in security is conditioned by the nature of the property secured. For example, whether the property is corporeal or heritable in nature dictates the form of the security.

Securities arising by operation of law

The nature of the security which emerges by operation of law is dependent on the form of property to which it relates. The two principal securities which arise by operation of law are lien (which may be special or general) and hypothec (eg landlord's hypothec). These securities are available to a creditor where it is in possession of the moveables of the debtor and the debtor has failed to make payment of a sum of money due to the creditor. In this chapter, we will analyse voluntary securities. Due to space constraints, we will not be examining securities arising by operation of law and you should consult your lecture notes here for revision purposes.

VOLUNTARY SECURITIES: RIGHTS IN SECURITY OVER CORPOREAL MOVEABLES

Introduction

Rights in security over corporeal moveables may be divided into possessory securities and non-possessory securities. Whilst a possessory security involves the owner/debtor relinquishing possession of its corporeal moveable assets to the creditor, a non-possessory security involves no transfer of possession from the owner/debtor to the creditor. Scots law has been traditionally hostile to the constitution of non-possessory rights in security. This hostility was and is based on the publicity principle of Scots property law which requires some form of publicity in connection with the creation or transfer of real rights. Since the constitution of rights in security over corporeal moveable assets involves the creation of real rights, such publicity is demanded by the law and delivery from the debtor to the lender is the traditional form of publicity required. However, over the past two centuries or so, a number of limited categories of non-possessory securities have been recognised by Scots law. The reason for the introduction of these limited forms of non-possessory security is tied up with the obvious impracticability of a debtor transferring possession of its moveable assets to creditors or lenders in the modern commercial climate. For example, a lender will not be particularly keen for its debtor customers to deliver their moveable assets (such as cranes, combine harvesters, JCB and other plant and machinery) to its offices. Moreover, the owner/debtor does not wish to be deprived of these moveable assets which it requires to carry on its ordinary day-to-day business. For that reason, Scots law has strived to enable debtors and creditors to constitute non-possessory forms of real rights in security over moveable assets as a means of recognising commercial reality.

Possessory securities: pledge

Introduction

Pledge is the main form of possessory security over corporeal moveables. The owner/debtor undertakes to pay the creditor or lender a sum of money and in security of that obligation duly grants a pledge which involves the transfer of certain identified moveable assets and property of the owner/debtor to the creditor or lender. If the owner/debtor fails to repay the sums owed, the creditor or lender may sell the property pledged to recover the balance of the sums owed.

Delivery

In *Pattison's Trustee* v *Liston* (1893), Lord Trayner stated that in order to validly constitute a pledge, delivery of the property which is the subject of the pledge is necessary. The case of *Bank of Scotland* v *Hutchison, Main & Co Ltd Liquidators* (1914) decided that an obligation on the owner/debtor to deliver the assets or property to the creditor or the lender is insufficient to create a pledge. Such an obligation merely confers a personal right in favour of the creditor or lender which does not defeat the claims of a trustee in sequestration or liquidator appointed over the estate of the owner/debtor. It is only when the real right in security of pledge is constituted by delivery that the rights of competing claimants to the assets of the debtor (such as a trustee in sequestration or liquidator appointed over the estate of the owner/debtor) will be defeated. Moreover, a sham sale entered into between the owner/debtor and creditor or lender (in terms of which the owner/debtor purports to "sell" his moveable assets to the creditor while holding on to possession and use of those assets in return for "payment" of a sum of money) is treated by Scots law as invalid as a right in security by virtue of *Allan* v *Galbraith* (1902) and as a sale by virtue of s 62(4) of the Sale of Goods Act 1979.

Forms of delivery

Whilst it is pivotal that delivery is required to constitute the pledge, it is not always the case that physical delivery is necessary. Delivery may be actual, symbolic or constructive. Actual delivery is straightforward to understand. Meanwhile, symbolic delivery entails the transfer of the documents of title to the assets to the creditor or lender, eg *Hayman* v *McLintock* (1907) where the owner/debtor delivered bills of lading in relation to certain goods to various creditors and lenders. Constructive delivery involves the intermediation of an independent third party keeper of assets owned by the owner/debtor. One example is where an independent third party keeping goods on behalf of the owner/debtor, eg a storekeeper, is given instructions by the owner/debtor to hold those assets or goods on behalf of the creditor or lender. The keeper must receive intimation of instructions from the owner/debtor. Otherwise, the case of *Inglis* v *Robertson & Baxter* (1898) stipulates that an effective pledge will not have been created.

Possessory securities: pawn

Another form of possessory security is the pawn under ss 8(1) and 189(1) of the Consumer Credit Act 1974. Any pledge given by a person who is not a body corporate in return for the provision of credit will constitute a pawn. Section 114(1) of the Consumer Credit Act 1974 stipulates that the creditor is under an obligation to give the owner/debtor a receipt in the prescribed form in exchange for the delivery of the items pawned and any failure to do so constitutes a criminal offence. In terms of ss 116 and 120(1)(b) of the Consumer Credit Act 1974, any item pawned is redeemable at any time within 6 months after it was taken, or such other longer period as the parties may agree. If the owner/debtor fails to redeem within this prescribed period, by virtue of the terms of s 116(3) of the Consumer Credit Act 1974, the owner/debtor continues to enjoy the right to redeem until the creditor sells the articles and realises the pawn. However, there is an exception which applies where the credit extended to the owner/debtor is £75 or less and the period of 6 months has expired. Here, s 120(1)(a) of the Consumer Credit Act 1974 directs that property in the items pawned passes automatically to the creditor at the end of that period. Section 117(1) of the Consumer Credit Act 1974 states that on the owner/debtor surrendering the pawn receipt and paying the amount owing, the creditor must redeliver the items pawned to the owner/debtor and the pawn is deemed to have been redeemed. Where the owner/debtor has misplaced or lost the pawn receipt, he may tender a statutory declaration in the prescribed form or a written statement (where the creditor agrees and the credit does not exceed £75) in accordance with s 118 of the Consumer Credit Act 1974. Section 121 of the Consumer Credit Act 1974 deals with the powers of the creditor to sell the articles pawned where the redemption period of 6 months or longer has expired. Here, it is stipulated that the creditor may sell the pawned articles after giving the owner/debtor not less than the prescribed period of notice of his intention to sell, indicating in the notice the asking price. Subsequent to the sale, the creditor must give the owner/debtor prescribed information in writing as to the sale, its proceeds and expenses. Where there is a surplus in the proceeds of sale vis-à-vis the sum owing, then the debt secured by the pawn is discharged and any surplus must be paid by the creditor to the owner/debtor.

Non-possessory securities: introduction

Scots common law was traditionally unsympathetic to the recognition of non-possessory forms of security over the corporeal moveable assets of a debtor. Over time, however, certain types were received into the law of Scotland. For example, for obvious reasons, it was recognised that it was impracticable for ships, sea-bearing vessels and cargo to be pledged, since it was plain that it would be more or less impossible to arrange for delivery of these moveables to the creditor. For that reason, Bell's *Principles*, ss 452–456 states that Scots common law recognised the bond of bottomry, which is a right in security granted over ships, and the bond of respondentia, which could be granted as security over a ship's cargo. The position with regard to ships is now governed by s 16 of the Merchant Shipping Act 1995, which provides for a statutory form of mortgage over ships or a share in ships without delivery or the transfer of possession to the creditor. Paragraph 7 of Sch 1 to the Merchant Shipping Act 1995 directs that the mortgage must be registered in the Register of British Shipping to be valid. It is equally possible to create statutory mortgages over registered aircraft in terms of s 86 of the Civil Aviation Act 1982 and the Mortgaging of Aircraft Order 1972 (SI 1972/1268).

Non-possessory securities: floating charge

Introduction

The floating charge is the most important non-possessory security which is available in terms of Scots law by virtue of s 38(1) of the Bankruptcy and Diligence etc (Scotland) Act 2007 ("BDA 2007"). A company, limited liability partnership, industrial and provident society or a European Economic Interest Grouping may grant such a charge in return for credit or a loan. When it is created, the floating charge hovers over all of the assets and undertaking of the granter. However, it does not confer a real right in security over any particular asset. Thus, the granter of the floating charge may sell and buy assets in the ordinary course of its business without obtaining the prior consent of the floating charge holder. However, when the charge crystallises (sometimes also referred to as attachment), it ceases to hover and instead attaches over all of the assets and undertaking of the granter stipulated to be secured in terms of the floating charge instrument (in practice, it is standard for the floating charge instrument to state that all of the assets and undertaking of the granter are subject to the floating charge). The effect of crystallisation is that the charge is treated as if it was a fixed security over the property of the granter and those assets are available to a liquidator, receiver or administrator to ingather and sell in order to make good the sums owing to creditors. The charge crystallises on the appointment of a liquidator (in terms of s 45(1) of the BDA 2007), the appointment of a receiver (in terms of s 53(7) of the Insolvency Act 1986) or on an administrator filing a notice to the effect that he thinks that the company has insufficient property to enable a distribution to be made to the company's unsecured creditors (by virtue of para 115(3) of Sch B1 to the Insolvency Act 1986).

Constitution

The provisions of s 38(3) of the BDA 2007 state that a floating charge must be executed as a deed and registered in the Register of Floating Charges in order to be effective. Otherwise, the charge is invalid. It is possible to take advantage of an advance notice procedure. In terms of s 39 of the BDA 2007, where a company proposes to grant a floating charge, the company and the person in whose favour the charge is to be granted may apply to have joint notice of the proposed charge registered in the Register of Floating Charges. Provided the floating charge instrument is registered within 21 days of the date of registration of the advance notice, the floating charge is treated as having been created when the notice was registered, ie the date of registration is backdated to the date of the registration of the notice.

Ranking

Floating charges and other real rights in security (such as a pledge or a standard security over heritage) rank in accordance with the date of their creation. A floating charge is created when it is registered in the Register of Floating Charges, whilst a fixed security is created on the date that it is constituted as a real right. In the case of a pledge, the date of creation will be the date of delivery. The date of creation of a standard security is the date on which the standard security is registered in the Land Register. Thus, if a standard security is registered in the Land Register on 16 November, a floating charge is registered in the Register of Floating Charges on 18 November and a second floating charge is registered on 19 November, the standard security will rank in priority to the two floating charges and the first floating charge will rank in priority to the second floating charge. However, it is possible for the floating charge holders and fixed security holders to change the priority of ranking within a floating charge or standard security instrument. For example, in the example given above, it is open to the holder of floating charge number 1 to agree with the granter of the charge that it will take priority over the standard security which was created earlier. However, s 41(4) of the BDA 2007 states that the agreement of all charge holders affected is required and so, in the example given above, this would mean that the consent and agreement of the holder of the standard security and the holder of the second charge to the postponement of that security would be required. This agreement may be set out in writing and registered in the Register of Floating Charges by virtue of s 41(5) of the BDA 2007. It is also possible for the ranking of charges and securities to be reordered by each holder of a security and charge entering into a document of alteration with the granter in accordance with s 43 of the BDA 2007. Such documents of alteration are better known as "ranking agreements". In order to be valid, they must be signed by the granter and each charge holder and/or security holder affected and registered against each floating charge and fixed security which they affect in terms of s 43(3) of the BDA 2007.

VOLUNTARY SECURITIES: RIGHTS IN SECURITY OVER INCORPOREAL MOVEABLES

Introduction

A debtor may grant a fixed security over incorporeal moveables which he owns, eg shares, patents, copyright, trade marks, debts and other accounts receivable, etc. Some incorporeal moveables are incapable of being secured such as alimentary rights and rights involving *delectus personae*.

Constitution

A fixed security over incorporeal movables is effected by the debtor transferring title to the creditor or lender under a document referred to as an assignation. Thus, title is actually assigned from the debtor to the creditor or lender. Assignation is the first stage in the constitution of the real right in security fixed over the specified incorporeal moveable property and is effective to confer a personal right in favour of the creditor or lender. The second stage entails intimation of the assignation to the account debtor in the relevant obligation and it is this second stage that functions to confer a real right in security over the secured asset in favour of the creditor/lender. The account debtor in the case of an insurance policy will be the insurance company, and in the case of debts and accounts receivable owed to the debtor, the third-party debtor who is due to pay such sums to the debtor.

Intimation

Without intimation, which is the equivalent of delivery (in the case of corporeal moveables), no real right in security will be created in favour of the creditor or lender as assignee. Thus, intimation is required to complete the right of the creditor or lender as assignee. If the creditor or lender has had an incorporeal moveable assigned to them without intimation, then all they have is a personal right in the incorporeal moveable asset secured and their interests are susceptible to defeat by other interested third parties, eg liquidators, trustees in sequestration, etc. For that reason, intimation which creates the real right in security, is critically important. The Transmission of Moveable Property (Scotland) Act 1862 provides for forms of assignation and intimation. However, it is not an absolute requirement that these forms be followed and more informal methods of effecting an assignation or intimation are permitted by Scots law. The principal question is whether the facts and circumstances of the particular case demonstrate that intimation has been made. For example, in the case of *Carter* v *McIntosh* (1862), it was held that a clear intention to assign at the present time was sufficient. Furthermore, intimation to the third party account debtor may be made in writing and the legal equivalent of a formal intimation will be implied by the law in certain circumstances, eg where it is unrealistic to suggest that the third party account debtor is unaware of the fact of the assignation. Examples include effecting diligence (Erskine, *Institute*, III, 5, 4) over the assets of the third party account debtor or the raising of court action against him (*Whyte* v *Neish* (1622)). Once the intimation has been sent, there is no requirement that the third party account debtor must acknowledge it for valid intimation to have been made (*Christie Owen & Davies plc t/a Christie & Co* v *Campbell* (2009)). Moreover, the third party account debtor may be personally barred from arguing that intimation has not been effected where he has previously promised to make payment to the assignee (*Home and Elphinstone* v *Murray* (1674)). Since it is critical to intimate to a third party account debtor the existence of the assignation in order to create the real right in security, it follows that it is not possible to effect a real right in security over the property of the owner/debtor that does not exist or that is not owned by the owner/debtor at the point in time at which the attempt was made to effect the intimation. Thus, a *spes successionis* may not be secured.

Impossibility of intimation

On occasion, intimation will be impossible. Where the incorporeal moveables being secured are shares, patents, copyright or trade marks, there will be no account debtor to whom intimation may be made, since these rights do not involve corresponding obligations or duties on the part of third party account debtors to make payment or otherwise. In the case of shares, patents or trade marks, the constitution of the real right in security will be effected by registration and so registration performs the role of intimation. In the case of shares, registration in the company's register of members is required to perfect the real right in security over the shares in favour of the creditor or lender (*Guild* v *Young* (1884)). Meanwhile, in the case of patents or trade marks, ss 31–33 of the Patents Act 1977 and ss 22–24 of the Trade Marks Act 1994 stipulate that registration is required in order to create the real right in security. Finally, there is no register of copyrights and thus s 90 of the Copyright, Designs and Patents Act 1988 directs that an assignation without intimation or registration is sufficient to confer a real right in security in favour of a creditor or lender.

Assignatus utitur iure auctoris

Once the real right in security over the incorporeal moveable property has been constituted in favour of the creditor or lender, the principle of *assignatus utitur iure auctoris* applies to condition the extent of the creditor or lender's rights. This principle holds that the assignee, ie the creditor or lender, obtains no better right than the cedent/assignor, ie the debtor. Thus, if the account debtor has a defence to the claim of the cedent/assignor, that defence is also available to the account debtor against the claim of the assignee, ie the creditor or lender. One can conceptualise the principle of *assignatus utitur iure auctoris* as being concerned with the enforcement of the real right in security by the creditor or lender. The case of *Shiells* v *Ferguson, Davidson & Co* (1876) provides a good example of the rule in operation. Here, the debt assigned in security from the debtor to the creditor had been extinguished by virtue of the operation of compensation (a form of set-off of money claims) prior to the perfection of the assignation in security. Since this had occurred, the creditor's security was worthless and could not be enforced against the account debtor.

VOLUNTARY SECURITIES: RIGHTS IN SECURITY OVER HERITAGE

Introduction

A debtor may create a real right in security over his heritable property, ie land or buildings. Where a creditor takes a standard security, he is referred to as the "heritable creditor". Section 9(3) of the Conveyancing and Feudal Reform (Scotland) Act 1970 ("the 1970 Act") directs that the standard security is the only competent security which can be granted in security over land or real right in land to a creditor or lender for the purpose of securing a debt. In terms of s 9(8)(c) of the 1970 Act, the definition of "debt" is wide enough to encompass obligations to repay fixed and fluctuating sums of money, non-monetary obligations *ad factum praestandum* (which enjoin a person to undertake a particular task) and annuities. However, rent and other periodical sums payable in respect of land are expressly excluded. The standard security over any land or real right in land may be registered in the Register of Sasines or Land Register and the meaning of a "real right in land" is set out in s 9(8)(b) of the 1970 Act. Once recorded or registered in the Register of Sasines or Land Register, a standard security will confer a real right in security in favour of the creditor in terms of s 11(1) of the 1970 Act.

Form of standard security

Section 9(2) of the 1970 Act directs that the standard security must conform with one of the prescribed forms set out in Sch 2 to the 1970 Act. Form A ought to be used where the personal obligation to repay the debt is included in the standard security instrument and Form B where the personal obligation is not so included.

Standard conditions

The 1970 Act contains standard conditions which govern the relationship between the debtor and the heritable creditor and the powers and rights of the latter. Section 11(2) of the 1970 Act provides that the standard conditions outlined in Sch 3 to the 1970 Act are incorporated into every standard security, unless varied in accordance with the provisions of s 11(3) of the 1970 Act. Section 11(3) directs that some of the standard conditions may not be varied, namely the conditions relating to redemption, powers of sale and foreclosure. The standard conditions delimited in Sch 3 comprise 12 separate conditions. Condition 1 imposes obligations of maintenance and repair on the debtor, while condition 2 stipulates that the debtor is obliged to complete any unfinished buildings to the satisfaction of the creditor. The other conditions impose obligations on the debtor to perform all monetary and non-monetary obligations in respect of the land, eg to pay rates and other land taxes, to insure the buildings, to comply with planning obligations and to refrain from letting the subjects secured. The latter condition not to let or sub-let the secured property is particularly important, since the case of *Trade Development Bank* v *Warriner and Mason (Scotland) Ltd* (1980) demonstrates that a tenant's lease of the secured heritable property can be reduced by the creditor, unless the creditor had knowledge that the tenant had a real right of lease at the time when the security was granted. Condition 7 provides the creditor with the power to perform obligations which the debtor has failed to perform in terms of the standard conditions and to charge the debtor for the costs of performance of such obligations. Condition 8 empowers the creditor to "call up" the standard security in accordance with the provisions of s 19 of the 1970 Act, ie to take action to enforce the standard security in order to recoup the indebtedness of the debtor to the creditor. Condition 9 states that a debtor is held to be in default of his obligations when a calling-up notice has been served but not complied with, when he has failed to comply with any other requirement of the standard security or when the proprietor of the security (usually the debtor) has become insolvent. Condition 10 regulates the rights of the creditor on the debtor's default and condition 11 sets out the rules with regard to the right of the debtor to exercise its right to redeem the standard security. Finally, condition 12 specifies that the debtor is liable for the costs of preparing and recording or registering the standard security.

Ranking

Section 13 of the 1970 Act applies to regulate the priority of standard securities where more than one has been granted. The general rule in s 13(1) of the 1970 Act is that standard securities rank in accordance with the date of recording or registration. However, in terms of *Scotlife Homes (No 2) Ltd* v *Muir* (1994), it is open to the parties to regulate the order of priority by agreement and such agreement is usually manifested by (i) a negative pledge clause in the standard security, or (ii) a ranking agreement. Section 13(1) of the 1970 Act stipulates that where a first ranking standard security holder receives notice of the creation of a subsequent ranking standard security, the first ranking standard security is restricted to (a) the original debt incurred, (b) any further advances which the creditor is under a contractual obligation to make, (c) interest chargeable on such advances, and (d) any expenses or outlays reasonably incurred in the exercise of any power conferred by the security.

Competitions

Where a creditor holds some other security from the debtor, eg a creditor who has undertaken diligence or has sought to do so, the holder of the standard security will find itself engaged in a competition. In the event that the debtor has been inhibited prior to the debtor granting the standard security to the creditor, the inhibition will defeat the right of the creditor in the standard security (*Baird and Brown* v *Stirrat's Tr* (1872)). However, where the inhibition is effected after the grant of a standard security, the standard security will take precedence over the inhibition (*Campbell's Trs* v *De Lisle's Exrs* (1870)).

When the debtor enters into sequestration, liquidation, receivership or administration, the rights of the secured creditor in terms of the standard security will be preserved. Thus, since the standard security is a fixed security, the trustee in sequestration, liquidator, receiver or administrator will be required to obtain the consent of the holder of the standard security prior to sale of the secured property or seek the authority of the court to sell. Moreover, the secured creditor will be paid out in priority to unsecured creditors on the distribution of the estate by the trustee in sequestration, liquidator, receiver or administrator to the creditors.

Discharge

The relevant rules governing discharge are contained in s 17 of the 1970 Act. The secured property may be disburdened from the standard security by the recording of a discharge in terms of the prescribed forms in Sch 4 to the 1970 Act. Of course, the creditor will only consent to, and execute, such a discharge if it is satisfied that the outstanding indebtedness owed by the debtor has been repaid in full. Subject to agreement to the contrary, s 18 of the 1970 Act and standard condition 11 regulate the redemption of standard securities. Here, it is directed that the debtor is entitled to redeem the security on giving 2 months' notice of his intention to do so and in accordance with the prescribed forms set out in Sch 5 to the Act. The redemption notice may be given by the debtor, or his successors in title, assignees or representatives to the creditor, or his successors in title, assignees or representatives.

Enforcement

There are two options open to a creditor holding a standard security where it wishes to enforce the standard security. The first is to serve a default notice upon the debtor in conformity with Form B of Sch 6 to the 1970 Act in terms of s 21 of the 1970 Act and standard condition 9. The second option is to serve a calling-up notice upon the proprietor of the subjects secured under the standard security (usually the debtor) in conformity with Form A of Sch 6 to the 1970 Act under s 19 of the 1970 Act. However, where the proprietor of the subjects secured by the standard security becomes insolvent, the effect of standard condition 9(1)(c) is that the creditor must serve a calling-up notice.

Default notice

A default notice may be served where the debtor breaches an obligation arising out of the security and the default may be remedied. Here, the creditor may serve the default notice calling on the debtor to purge/remedy the default (ie pay the sums due) within a period of 1 month. Default is defined in standard condition 9(1). A debtor is held to be in default of his obligations when a calling-up notice has been served upon him and has not been complied with, when he has failed to comply with any other requirement of the standard security or when the proprietor (usually the debtor) has become insolvent. By virtue of s 22 of the 1970 Act, the debtor has a period of 14 days to object to the notice to the court. The court may uphold the objection, vary it or set it aside in whole or in part. The consequences of the debtor failing to comply with the default notice are spelt out in standard condition 10. It is stipulated that the creditor may sell, carry out necessary repairs or apply to the court for a decree of foreclosure.

Calling-up notice

The main objective of the creditor in serving a calling-up notice is to exercise the power of sale which is available under the 1970 Act. For that reason, it is more attractive to the creditor seeking to enforce the standard security. However, the period of notice is longer in the case of a calling-up notice. The calling-up notice must give the debtor a period of 2 months to pay. Where the debtor fails to comply with the calling-up notice, the creditor is entitled to exercise the statutory default powers which are set out in standard condition 10(2)–(7) in terms of s 24 of the 1970 Act, namely the power of sale, the power to enter into possession of the secured subjects and receive or recover the rents of those subjects, the power to let the secured subjects or any part thereof, the power to carry out necessary repairs and the power to apply to the court for a decree of foreclosure.

Powers under standard condition 10(2)–(7)

When exercising the power of sale, the creditor must take into account the interests of the debtor. Therefore, where the proceeds of the sale of the security subjects exceed the level of the outstanding indebtedness, the creditor must account to the debtor for the surplus. Section 25 of the 1970 Act stipulates that the creditor may sell by private bargain or public roup (ie auction) and the creditor is under a duty to advertise the sale and to take all reasonable steps to ensure that the price at which the subjects or any part are sold is the best that can reasonably be obtained. The creditor may be liable in damages to the debtor where it breaches its duties under s 25 of the 1970 Act (*Royal Bank of Scotland* v *A and M Johnston* (1987) and *Bank of Credit* v *Thompson* (1987)). However, it is evidentially very difficult for a debtor to satisfy the court that the creditor has breached such duties (*Dick* v *Clydesdale Bank plc* (1991)). Once the secured property has been sold by the creditor, the proceeds of sale must be distributed in accordance with s 27 of the 1970 Act, namely: first, the expenses of the sale must be paid; secondly, sums which are due under other any prior security to which the sale was not made subject; thirdly, any sums due under the standard security and other securities of equal ranking; and, finally, sums due under securities which are postponed to the standard security in accordance with their ranking.

The creditor also has a default power to recover any rents due from tenants of the secured subjects from the date the creditor enters possession, but not arrears of rent (*UCB Bank Ltd* v *Hire Foulis (in Liquidation)* (1999)). The other default power of the creditor which is extremely important is the right of foreclosure, ie standard condition 10(7). The foreclosure right enables the creditor to take ownership of the secured subjects. Section 28 of the 1970 Act stipulates conditions for the exercise of the right of foreclosure. Section 28(5) of the 1970 Act states that the effect of the recording of a decree of foreclosure is that the creditor is vested in the subjects, the debtor's right to redeem the standard security is extinguished, the subjects are disburdened of any standard security and all other postponed securities and diligences and the creditor is given the same right as the debtor to redeem any security ranking prior to, or equally with, his own security.

Residential subjects

Where the subjects secured are used to any extent for residential purposes, the Mortgage Rights (Scotland) Act 2001 ("the 2001 Act") will apply to curtail the ability of the creditor to exercise the statutory default powers which are set out in standard condition 10(2)–(7) on the breach of a default notice or calling-up notice. Section 1 of the 2001 Act narrates that enforcement action taken by a creditor under a standard security may be suspended where a calling-up notice or default notice has been served or an application has been made to the court under s 24 of the 1970 Act. In terms of s 1(2)–(4) of the 2001 Act, the application for suspension of enforcement action may be made by the debtor, the proprietor of the subjects and certain other persons. The application must be made to the court before the expiry of the period specified in the default notice or the calling-up notice or before the conclusion of proceedings raised under s 24 of the 1970 Act. The effect of an application made under s 1(1) of the 2001 Act is that the creditor's rights under the 1970 Act are suspended pending the determination of the application by the court. Section 2(2) of the 2001 Act sets out the criteria which the court must consider when it is deciding whether to make an order to permanently suspend the creditor's rights under condition 10.

Essential Facts

- Rights in security may confer personal or real rights in favour of a creditor.
- Real rights in security confer rights in security in favour of a creditor over the property and assets of a person.
- Rights in security are accessory to the primary right of the trader or lender to be paid or to have the loan repaid.
- Real rights in security may be voluntary or arise by operation of law.

- Real rights in security may be fixed or floating.
- Pledge and pawn are two real rights in security which a creditor may take over the corporeal assets of a debtor or third party.
- A floating charge is a form of non-possessory right in security which is not fixed over any of the assets of the debtor. It becomes fixed only on the occurrence of crystallisation.
- Rights in security are constituted over incorporeal moveables by assignation and intimation or registration.
- Intimation will be effective where the facts and circumstances of the particular case demonstrate that intimation has been made to the third party account debtor.
- A standard security is the only form of right in security available over heritage.
- The Conveyancing and Feudal Reform (Scotland) Act 1970 regulates the constitution, ranking, discharge and enforcement of standard securities.

Essential Cases

Pattison's Tr v Liston (1893): in order to validly constitute a pledge, delivery of the property which is the subject of the pledge is necessary.

Bank of Scotland v Hutchison, Main & Co Ltd Liquidators (1914): an obligation on the owner/debtor to deliver the assets or property to the creditor or the lender is insufficient to create a pledge.

Hayman v McLintock (1907): symbolic delivery entails the transfer of the documents of title to the assets to the creditor or lender.

Inglis v Robertson & Baxter (1898): where a storekeeper is not given instructions by the owner/debtor to hold particular assets or goods on behalf of the creditor or lender, constructive delivery will not have taken place in order to validly create a pledge.

Carter v McIntosh (1862): a clear intention to assign at the present time was sufficient to constitute sufficient intimation.

Christie Owen & Davies plc t/a Christie & Co v Campbell (2009): once a letter of intimation has been sent, there is no requirement that the third party account debtor must acknowledge it for valid intimation to have been made.

Home and Elphinstone v Murray (1674): a third party account debtor may be personally barred from arguing that intimation has not been effected where they have previously promised to make payment to the assignee.

Shiells v Ferguson, Davidson & Co (1876): an example of *assignatus utitur iure auctoris* in operation.

Trade Development Bank v Warriner and Mason (Scotland) Ltd (1980): where a debtor has granted a standard security to a heritable creditor and fails to inform the creditor that the subjects secured have been let to a tenant, the tenant's lease can be reduced by the creditor, unless the creditor had knowledge that the tenant had a real right of lease at the time when the security was granted.

Baird and Brown v Stirrat's Tr (1872): in a competition between an inhibitor and a heritable creditor, the standard security will not cut down the inhibition where the former was effected prior to the constitution of the latter.

Campbell's Trs v De Lisle's Exrs (1870): where an inhibition is effected after the grant of a standard security, the standard security will take precedence over the inhibition.

6 CAUTIONARY OBLIGATIONS

At the beginning of Chapter 5 on rights in security, consideration was given to the distinction between personal and real rights which function to provide security to a creditor or lender. That chapter moved on to examine real rights and obligations in security. In this chapter, we will explore personal rights and obligations in more detail. The adjective attached to these rights and obligations underscores that they are personal. That is to say that they are not enforceable over an identified item of property. Instead, the obligation to make good the debt owed to the creditor is imposed on a legal person such as an individual, partnership or company. The law refers to that third party as a cautioner and the obligations imposed on that cautioner are referred to as cautionary obligations. In a layperson's terms, the cautionary obligation is a guarantee and the cautioner is a guarantor.

PARTIES

The law of caution involves three parties. First, there is the principal debtor who has a personal obligation to pay sums to the second party, namely the creditor. There will usually be a contract between the principal debtor and the creditor recognising this personal obligation. However, such a contract is not essential. The arrangement usually entails a separate contract between the creditor and the cautioner known as a contract of cautionry. Such contract provides that the cautioner will pay a certain sum of money (usually the principal debt, plus interest on that sum and the creditor's costs and expenses) or perform a particular obligation in the event that the principal debtor fails to pay such sum or perform such obligation. It is precisely that obligation which burdens the cautioner, which is referred to as the cautionary obligation. The cautionary obligation is accessory in nature in the sense that it rests on the principal obligation of the principal debtor. Therefore, the common law rule is that the cautionary obligation is not an independent obligation and, generally, for the cautionary obligation to continue in existence, there must be an independent principal obligation. However, there is an exception whereby the principal obligation need not exist when the cautionary obligation is entered into, so long as it is contemplated in the future.

CONSTITUTION AND FORM OF CAUTIONARY OBLIGATIONS

Writing

Cautionary obligations do not require to be committed to writing in order to be validly constituted. However, there is one exception where writing is required in terms of s 1(2)(a)(ii) of the Requirements of Writing (Scotland) Act 1995. Here, it is stipulated that writing is required for the proper constitution of a cautionary obligation where it is a gratuitous unilateral obligation not undertaken in the course of a business. Where the cautionary obligation amounts to a security or guarantee for a regulated agreement under the Consumer Credit Act 1974 ("the 1974 Act"), s 105(1) of the 1974 Act states that it must be in writing and executed by the cautioner.

Other requirements

Subject to the above, a contract of cautionry can be constituted in the same way as any contract, that is to say by offer and acceptance. However, acceptance is not always necessary, which is linked to the debate concerning whether cautionry is properly regarded as a contract or promise. For example, in the case of *Fortune* v *Young* (1918), the Court of Session ruled that where a cautioner gives a letter to a particular individual which makes a general offer to act as a cautioner to any third party creditor in respect of the debts or obligations of that particular individual as debtor, that offer is valid and may be enforced by any third party creditor duly acting on it. Furthermore, the case of *Wallace* v *Gibson* (1895) is an authority for the proposition that it is possible to constitute a cautionary obligation by the creditor acting on a cautioner's unconditional offer to give caution without the requirement for any prior acceptance on the part of the creditor before dealings are entered into with the debtor. It is also possible for there to be more than one cautioner. In such circumstances, the cautioners are known as co-cautioners.

ACCESSORY NATURE OF CAUTIONARY OBLIGATION

Introduction

A cautionary obligation is accessory in nature. Therefore, it is not an independent principal obligation which stands on its own and it cannot exist without linkage to an independent principal obligation between a debtor and a creditor. When the principal obligation is extinguished, so is the cautionary obligation (*Swan* v *Bank of Scotland* (1835)).

Distinction between cautionary obligation and indemnity

A particular difficulty is distinguishing a cautionary obligation from an independent principal obligation such as an indemnity. An indemnity is essentially an obligation by a party to make good a loss sustained by, or pay a sum of money to, a third party on the occurrence of a particular event. The factor which distinguishes an indemnity from a cautionary obligation is that the former is not accessory to an independent obligation to pay a principal debt. However, the problem is that sometimes the event which triggers the indemnity is the failure of a party to pay a debt to another party. In such circumstances, it is far from straightforward to ascertain the nature of the obligation to pay and whether it is an indemnity or a cautionary obligation. For example, consider how one distinguishes between the following scenarios: first, A enters into an independent principal obligation to pay £10,000 to B. C enters into a cautionary obligation to pay B £10,000 in the event that A fails to pay that sum to B. Secondly, A enters into an independent principal obligation to pay £10,000 to B. C agrees to indemnify B in the event that A fails to pay that sum to B. In the first example, the obligation owed by C to B is a cautionary obligation because it is stated to be so. However, in the second example, the obligation owed by C to B is categorised as an independent obligation, namely an indemnity. Again, the example states it is an indemnity. The difficulty, of course, is where the obligation is not specifically labelled as a cautionary obligation or an indemnity. The factor which the courts apply to distinguish between these similar transactions was expounded by Lord Esher MR in *Sutton & Co* v *Grey* (1894), where it was held that the existence of a connection between C in the above example and the independent obligation entered into between A and B is crucial. Where there is no such connection apart from the obligation on C to pay B, C's obligation will be deemed to be an indemnity. However, where there is such a connection, the obligation will be ruled to be cautionary in nature.

Distinction between cautionary obligation and other obligations

The case of *Stevenson's Trustee* v *Campbell & Sons* (1896) is an authority for the point that there is also a distinction between a cautionary obligation and the situation where an individual agrees to order goods for Z on the basis that that individual will pay for them. In the latter example, the principal obligation is imposed on the individual, rather than the individual acting in the capacity as cautioner for Z. Moreover, some documents which specifically state that they are guarantees are not in fact guarantees and so do not give rise to cautionary obligations. A prime example is the performance bond or performance guarantee where, in return for a fee, a bank obliges itself to make a payment to A in the event that B fails to fulfil its obligation(s) to A (*Cargill International SA* v *Bangladesh Sugar and Food Industries Corporation* (1998)).

Implications of obligation being cautionary in nature

Where an independent obligation is extinguished, the cautionary obligation falls. Whereas the extinction of an independent obligation does not affect the continuance or validity of an indemnity or obligation which is not cautionary (*Yeoman Credit Ltd* v *Latter* (1961)). Thus, it is crucial to distinguish between a cautionary obligation and an obligation that resembles a cautionary obligation which is in fact independent in nature.

PROPER AND IMPROPER CAUTIONRY

Bell's *Principles*, s 247 directs that a contract of proper cautionry is one in which it is *ex facie* evident from the express terms of the deed that a person is a cautioner. However, in the case of a contract of improper cautionry, there is the appearance that the cautioner and the principal debtor are joint co-debtors. Historically, the distinction was crucial since it was only a proper cautioner who was entitled to exercise the rights of discussion and division. The right of discussion is a cautioner's right to insist that the creditor takes all reasonable steps against the debtor to enforce payment of the debt through court action and diligence prior to seeking to enforce the payment of the debtor's debt against the cautioner in terms of the cautionary obligation. Section 8 of the Mercantile Law Amendment (Scotland) Act 1856, however, removed the right of discussion with an exception for circumstances where discussion is expressly provided for in the instrument of caution. The effect of this statutory provision is that a creditor does not need to discuss the debt before moving against the cautioner. Meanwhile, in terms of the right of division, each co-cautioner is liable for his pro rata share of the debtor's debt only. This can be contrasted with improper cautionry where co-cautioners are jointly and severally liable for the principal debt.

THE EFFECT OF MISREPRESENTATION, UNDUE INFLUENCE AND FACILITY AND CIRCUMVENTION ON THE CONTRACT OF CAUTIONRY

Misrepresentation

Where the creditor misrepresents matters to the cautioner and thus induces the cautioner to enter into the contract of cautionry, so long as that misrepresentation is material, the cases of *Smith* v *Bank of Scotland* (1829) and *Royal Bank of Scotland* v *Ranken* (1844) demonstrate that the cautionary obligation will be deemed to be void. This reflects the fact that a contract of cautionry is governed by general contractual principles. The rules on misrepresentation, however, do not lead to a separate rule that the creditor is under a positive duty to disclose material facts of which the cautioner was unaware, which if disclosed may have affected the cautioner's decision to enter into the cautionary obligation (*Young* v *Clydesdale Bank* (1889)).

Misrepresentation by debtor to, or undue influence by debtor over, the cautioner

In the case of a misrepresentation made by the debtor to the cautioner or the exertion of undue influence on the cautioner by the debtor, historically, the legal position was that the validity of the cautionary obligation would not be called into question except in circumstances where the creditor was aware of the misrepresentation or undue influence. However, the position changed when the House of Lords decided *Smith* v *Bank of Scotland* (1997). In *Smith*, a wife claimed that she had been induced to enter into a cautionary obligation in respect of the debts of her husband's business by virtue of a misrepresentation made to her by her husband and by the exertion of undue influence. The creditor was unaware of any misrepresentation or undue influence. Nevertheless, the House of Lords ruled that the doctrine of good faith imposes an obligation on a creditor to advise a prospective cautioner to take independent legal advice where the circumstances are such that a reasonable person would believe that, owing to the personal relationship between the debtor and the prospective cautioner, the consent of the latter may not be freely given or fully informed. Where the creditor fails in the obligation to direct the cautioner to obtain independent legal advice, he is not in good faith and so the cautionary obligation cannot be enforced. Relationships which are sufficiently close to the creditor to give rise to the good faith duty are husband and wife and, as shown in *Wright* v *Cotias Investments Inc* (2000), parent and child where the parent is acting as the cautioner.

Content of the creditor's "good faith" obligation

With regard to the content of the creditor's obligation, *Forsyth* v *Royal Bank of Scotland* (2000) provides that if the cautioner is separately legally advised, the creditor need not take any further steps. Thus, a practice has emerged whereby the creditor will insist that the cautioner takes separate legal advice. *Broadway* v *Clydesdale Bank plc (No 1)* (2000) held that if the creditor has *reasonable grounds* for believing that such independent legal advice has been taken by the cautioner, the creditor will have no further obligation.

THE CAUTIONER'S LIABILITY

The exposure of a cautioner in respect of his cautionary obligation is a matter of interpretation of the contract of cautionry itself. *Aitken's Trustees* v *Bank of Scotland* (1945) provides that a cautionary obligation will be construed *contra proferentem*, ie construed in favour of the cautioner and against the creditor. Where a cautioner enters into a cautionary obligation, the case of *Jackson* v *McIver* (1875) demonstates that the extent of his liability can never be greater than that of the debtor. However, pursuant to *Struthers* v *Dykes* (1847), the cautioner may be liable for the costs and expenses of the creditor in taking steps against the debtor to enforce the debt. Where a cautioner enters into a cautionary obligation which guarantees all of the advances to be made to a debtor but places a financial limit on the extent of that liability, the cautioner will not be liable for sums advanced by the creditor to the debtor after the date on which that financial limit is met.

Extent of caution

Caution may be continuing or limited in its scope. Where a cautionary obligation is continuing, the cautioner is liable for all sums which are outstanding by the debtor. This can be contrasted with a limited cautionary obligation where the cautioner's exposure is limited to a particular transaction or series of transactions. Whether a cautionary obligation is continuing or limited is a matter of interpretation of the relevant contract (*Caledonian Banking Co* v *Kennedy's Trustees* (1870)).

THE CAUTIONER'S RIGHTS

Cautioners have a right of relief, the right to demand an assignation of the rights under the debt from the creditor, the right to share in any security granted by the debtor to a co-cautioner and the right to rank in the bankruptcy or sequestration of the debtor's estate where the cautioner has paid the creditor in full. The right of relief entitles the cautioner to demand that the principal debtor relieve him of all liability incurred to the creditor. Where the contract is silent as to an express right of relief, Erskine, *Institute*, III, 3, 65 stipulates that the right will be implied as a consequence of the *actio mandati* which the cautioner has against the principal debtor. The right of relief also extends to the expenses which the cautioner incurred in paying the principal debt and interest paid to the creditor (*Smithy's Place Ltd* v *Blackadder* (1991)). The right of relief is also available where the debt is not yet due and the cautioner has not been called upon by the creditor to pay the principal debt (*Doig* v *Lawrie* (1903)).

Right of assignation

The cautioner's right of assignation, which is known as the *beneficium cedendarum actionum*, enables the cautioner to call on the creditor to assign the debt, any securities for it, including diligences done by the creditor. However, the *beneficium cedendarum actionum* does not apply to securities granted to the creditor by third parties (*Gordon's Trustees* v *Young* (1910)). This right is available to the cautioner once he has paid the principal debt in full and ensures that the cautioner steps into the shoes of the creditor. The purpose of this right is to enable the cautioner to enforce his right of relief against the debtor or against co-cautioners.

Right to share in security

The cautioner's right to share in any security granted by the debtor to a co-cautioner is also useful, but like the *beneficium cedendarum actionum* does not apply to securities granted by third parties (*Scott* v *Young* (1909)).

Right to rank in insolvency

Where the principal debtor becomes bankrupt and the cautioner pays the creditor in full, the cautioner will rank in the insolvency of the debtor as an ordinary creditor. Difficulties arise where the extent of the cautioner's liability extends to part only of the principal debt or where a limitation has been placed on the amount for which it is to be liable, and a larger debt has been incurred. Much depends on the construction of the contract since in the case of the former, the cautioner will be entitled to rank in respect of sums paid by the cautioner up to the limit, whereas, in the latter situation, the cautioner will not be entitled to rank.

TERMINATION OF THE CAUTIONARY OBLIGATION BY EXTINCTION OF THE PRINCIPAL DEBT

Since a cautionary obligation is accessory in nature, where the principal obligation is extinguished, the cautionary obligation is also extinguished. Thus, the cautioner's obligation is extinguished where the principal debtor is discharged from liability by the creditor without the cautioner's consent (*Aitken's Trustees* v *Bank of Scotland* (1945)).

Extinction by novation

A cautionary obligation may also be extinguished by the novation of the principal debt. Novation occurs where the principal debt is terminated and a new debt is constituted, ie one obligation is substituted for another. Where the identity of the principal debtor changes, ie the party owing the obligation is changed, the cautioner is released from his cautionary obligation. Novation is distinct from assignation since, in the case of an assignation, the obligation is one and the same and it is only the identity of the creditor which changes. In the case of assignation, the cautioner continues to be bound by his cautionary obligation (*Waydale Ltd* v *DHL Holdings (UK) Ltd (No 2)* (2001)).

Extinction by compensation or prescription

The exercise of compensation may also function to relieve a cautioner of his obligation. If the creditor is due money to the cautioner or the debtor when the creditor makes a demand against the cautioner for the payment of the principal debt, the operation of compensation may result in the extinction of the cautioner's obligation. Prescription of the principal obligation will also result in the extinction of the cautionary obligation.

Clayton's Case

In the context of a current account, the rule in *Clayton's Case* (*Devaynes* v *Noble, Clayton's Case* (1816)) may operate to extinguish the cautioner's liability. This rule provides that in the case of a current account between debtor and creditor, when a payment is made to account and there has been no appropriation of the payment by either the debtor or the creditor, the law will stipulate that payments to the credit side are applied to reduce items on the debit side in the chronological order in which they were incurred. When this rule is applied, the consequence is that the principal debt may be extinguished with the outcome that the cautioner is discharged.

TERMINATION OF THE CAUTIONARY OBLIGATION BY THE ACTIONS OF THE CREDITOR

The creditor's actions may be such that the law presumes that the cautioner is released from its cautionary obligation. There are certain well-recognised categories where the actions of the creditor are deemed to be consistent with such an intention to release the cautioner.

"Giving time"

The first category arises where the creditor binds himself to "give time" to the principal without the consent of the cautioner (*C & A Johnstone* v *Duthie* (1892)). The creditor will be deemed to have given the debtor time where the creditor agrees to postpone the time at which payment by the principal debtor is due.

Prejudicial alteration of contract between debtor and creditor

Secondly, the cautioner will be discharged if he is prejudiced, without his consent, by an alteration of the contract between the creditor and the principal debtor. For example, in the case of *N G Napier Ltd* v *Crosbie* (1964), the cautioner was released from liability where the principal debtor's weekly repayments of the principal were increased.

Discharge of co-cautioner

Thirdly, s 9 of the Mercantile Law Amendment (Scotland) Act 1856 directs that a joint cautioner will be discharged where the creditor discharges another joint co-cautioner without the consent of the joint cautioner. This section does not apply where the cautioner is not jointly liable with the co-cautioner and where both parties have guaranteed to repay a separate sum. A good example is the case of *Morgan* v *Smart* (1872) where a co-cautioner was liable for £70 of a guaranteed debt of £105.

The cautioner was liable to the extent of £35 where the co-cautioner had paid £70 and been discharged by the creditor.

Giving up of security

Finally, a cautioner will be discharged where the creditor voluntarily gives up a security by releasing the cautioner to the value of that security.

TERMINATION OF THE CAUTIONARY OBLIGATION BY THE CAUTIONER AND BY OPERATION OF LAW

No unilateral revocation

The general rule is that a cautioner is not entitled to release himself from his cautionary obligation by unilateral revocation if he is guaranteeing a specific obligation. However, where the guarantee is continuing and no period of time is specified, *Buchanan* v *Main* (1900) demonstrates that the cautioner may, in the absence of an express provision precluding revocation, withdraw as to future advances by giving notice to the creditor.

Operation of express term

A cautionary obligation may also determine by operation of the express terms of the contract: eg where the guarantee is for a fixed term or for a specific transaction only, the expiry of that fixed term or the completion of that transaction will discharge the cautioner in respect of future liabilities to the creditor.

Death of debtor or creditor

Moreover, the death of the debtor or the creditor will discharge the cautioner from performance in respect of future advances. However, the cautioner will remain liable for existing sums due. If the cautioner dies, this does not discharge him from performance. His executor will be liable to make good the cautionary obligation.

Prescription

Finally, a cautionary obligation may be extinguished by prescription in terms of s 6(1)–(3) of the Prescription and Limitation (Scotland) Act 1973 where 5 years have elapsed since it became enforceable and no relevant claim or no acknowledgment of the existence of the obligation has been made during that period.

Essential Facts

- A contract of cautionry will provide that the cautioner will pay a certain sum of money (usually the principal debt, plus interest on that sum and the creditor's costs and expenses) or perform a particular obligation in the event that the principal debtor fails to pay such sum or perform such obligation.

- A cautionary obligation is accessory to the principal obligation in the sense that it rests on the principal obligation of the principal debtor.

- Subject to s 1(2)(a)(ii) of the Requirements of Writing (Scotland) Act 1995 and s 105(1) of the Consumer Credit Act 1974, cautionary obligations do not require to be committed to writing in order to be validly constituted.

- Offer and acceptance is not always necessary in order to form a contract of cautionry.

- A cautionary obligation is distinct from an indemnity, the latter being an independent primary obligation.

- Where an independent obligation is extinguished, the cautionary obligation falls.

- A cautionary obligation may be proper or improper.

- The doctrine of good faith imposes an obligation on a creditor to advise a prospective cautioner to take independent legal advice where the circumstances are such that a reasonable person would believe that, owing to the personal relationship between the debtor and the prospective cautioner, the consent of the latter may not be freely given or fully informed.

- A cautionary obligation will be construed *contra proferentem*, ie in favour of the cautioner and against the creditor.

- Cautioners have a right of relief, the right to demand an assignation from the creditor, the right to share in any security granted by the debtor to a co-cautioner and the right to rank in the bankruptcy or sequestration of the debtor's estate where the cautioner has paid the creditor in full.

- A cautionary obligation may be extinguished by the actions of the creditor, by the cautioner or by operation of law.

Essential Cases

Fortune v Young (1918): where a cautioner gives a letter to a particular individual which makes a general offer to act as a cautioner to any third party creditor in respect of the debts or obligations of that particular individual as debtor, that offer amounts to a cautionary obligation when acted upon.

Wallace v Gibson (1895): a cautionary obligation may be constituted by the creditor acting on a cautioner's unconditional offer to give caution without the requirement for any prior acceptance on the part of the creditor before dealings are entered into with the debtor.

Swan v Bank of Scotland (1835): when the principal obligation is extinguished, so is the cautionary obligation.

Sutton & Co v Grey (1894): establishes the criterion for distinguishing between a cautionary obligation and an independent obligation (eg an indemnity).

Cargill International SA v Bangladesh Sugar and Food Industries Corp (1998): a performance bond or performance guarantee is not a cautionary obligation.

Smith v Bank of Scotland (1829) and **Royal Bank of Scotland v Ranken (1844)**: where the creditor misrepresents matters to the cautioner, the cautionary obligation will be deemed to be void.

Smith v Bank of Scotland (1997): the doctrine of good faith imposes an obligation on a creditor to advise a prospective cautioner to take independent legal advice where the circumstances are such that a reasonable person would believe that, owing to the personal relationship between the debtor and the prospective cautioner, the consent of the latter may not be freely given or fully informed.

Broadway v Clydesdale Bank plc (No 1) (2000): if the creditor has *reasonable grounds* to believe that the cautioner has taken independent legal advice, the creditor will have no further obligation in order to discharge its duties under *Smith* v *Bank of Scotland* (1997).

Aitken's Trustees v Bank of Scotland (1945): a cautionary obligation will be construed *contra proferentem*.

Jackson v McIver (1875): the cautioner's liability can never be greater than that of the debtor.

Aitken's Trustees v Bank of Scotland (1945): the cautioner's obligation is extinguished where the principal debtor is discharged from liability by the creditor without the cautioner's consent.

C & A Johnstone v Duthie (1892): where the creditor binds himself to "give time" to the principal debtor without the consent of the cautioner, this may extinguish the cautionary obligation.

N G Napier Ltd v Crosbie (1964): the cautioner will be discharged from his cautionary obligation if he is prejudiced, without his consent, by an alteration of the contract between the creditor and the principal debtor.

7 NEGOTIABLE INSTRUMENTS

A negotiable instrument is a piece of paper which confers a right in favour of the owner to the payment of a sum of money. The amount of money is represented on the face of the document and so it is representative of a right of the owner of the instrument to be paid a debt from a third party. Ownership of the bill/document is transferred by indorsement and delivery or, in the case of some documents, delivery only.

Negotiability

The key matter which distinguishes the negotiable instrument from other forms of incorporeal moveable property representing a right to be paid a debt (a negotiable instrument is a form of incorporeal moveable property) is that the *nemo dat quod non habet* and *tantum et tale* rules do not apply where the transferee of the negotiable instrument pays value for the document and is in good faith. Rather than being transferred by assignation, a negotiable instrument is transferred by negotiation. Negotiability is extremely beneficial to a transferee. Once the instrument is transferred for value by A to B, provided B is in good faith, the effect of transfer by negotiation is that B will take the instrument free from any defects or flaws in A's title to the instrument. Hence, in terms of the legal concept of negotiation, B will take a better title to the instrument than A had at the point of transfer. This can be contrasted with the transfer of a debt from A to B by assignation. In such circumstances, even where B pays value to A and takes title to be paid the debt from A in good faith, any rights or defences which third parties, including the account debtor (ie the party due to pay the debt to A), have against A will also be good against B after the assignation.

Differences in transfer by negotiation and assignation

Another key difference between transfer by negotiation and assignation is that in the case of the former there is no requirement for (1) intimation of the transfer of the debt from A to B to be made to the account debtor or (2) a separate document of transfer (*Connal & Co v Loder* (1868)). Negotiation is what distinguishes a negotiable instrument from other property which establishes the right to be paid a debt. For example, a contractual right to be paid a debt pursuant to a bill of lading (*Kum v Wah Tat Bank* (1971)), an

IOU (*Muir* v *Muir* (1912)) and a building society withdrawal form (*Weir* v *National Westminster Bank* (1994)) are not negotiable instruments, since the sum of money represented by such pieces of paper are not transferable by indorsement and delivery, nor do they confer a better title on the transferee than that wielded by the transferor. The most common well-recognised forms of negotiable instrument are bills of exchange, cheques, sterling paper notes, promissory notes, bankers' drafts and Government Treasury bills.

Scope of chapter

This chapter will consider bills of exchange only.

BILLS OF EXCHANGE

Introduction

A bill of exchange is a form of negotiable instrument developed by commercial merchants in Medieval Europe. Instead of carrying cash and notes long distances, bills of exchange could be carried across borders and drawn on banks in different cities across Europe, whereupon the banks would make payment to the holder of the negotiable instrument in terms of the instructions on the bill itself. The beauty of the bill is that it could be transferred to a third party by negotiation as well as drawn on an identified bank. Originally, bills of exchange were regulated by the *lex mercatoria* (law merchant). However, the law governing bills of exchange is now found in the Bills of Exchange Act 1882 ("the 1882 Act").

Identity of parties

Within the 1882 Act, the relevant parties are referred to as the drawer, drawee, payee and indorsee. The drawer is the party who issues the bill and orders the drawee to make payment to the payee or the indorsee. The payee is the party in whose favour the bill is initially drawn and the drawee is the party on whom the bill is drawn and who is instructed by the drawer to pay the payee. So, for example, if the Bank of Belgium issues a bill of exchange to Jonathan instructing the Bank of Perthshire to pay Jonathan £10,000 on the presentation of the bill, the Bank of Belgium is the drawer, the Bank of Perthshire the drawee and Jonathan is the payee. The drawee, ie the Bank of Perthshire, accepts liability on the bill by signing the front of the bill when it is presented by Jonathan and then paying over the requisite sum of money to Jonathan. At this point, the drawee, ie the Bank of Perthshire, becomes the acceptor.

If Jonathan sells the bill to Didier by indorsing ("indorsation") and delivering it (ie he negotiates the bill in favour of Didier) to Didier before it is presented to the drawee, ie the Bank of Perthshire, Didier will become the indorsee. Indorsation is achieved by the payee signing the back of the bill of exchange in favour of the indorsee, eg when Didier pays Jonathan a sum of money representing the sum stated on the bill (usually at a discount), Jonathan will then sign over the bill to Didier by indorsing his signature on the back of the bill and naming Didier as the indorsee. Didier then has the option to present the bill to the Bank of Perthshire or do the same as Jonathan and indorse the bill on to another third party in return for payment. In this way, bills of exchange may be transferred a number of times before finally being drawn on the drawee.

Definition of "bill of exchange"

Section 3(1) of the 1882 Act defines a bill of exchange as "an unconditional order in writing, addressed by one person to another, signed by the person giving it, requiring the person to whom it is addressed to pay on demand, or at a fixed or determinable future time, a sum certain in money to or to the order of a specified person, or to the bearer." Each of these components must be satisfied in order for a document to qualify as a bill of exchange. It is worth noting that there is no requirement for the bill to be dated when it is issued. Each of the individual elements of the definition in s 3(1) of the 1882 Act will now be considered.

An "unconditional order"

First, the document must amount to "an unconditional order" on its face. The words "please pay" are satisfactory, but "we hereby authorise you to pay" in the case of *Hamilton* v *Spottiswoode* (1849) did not satisfy the definition.

Writing

Secondly, the unconditional order must be made "in writing". Section 2 of the 1882 Act directs that "written" includes printed and "writing" includes print. In the case of *Geary* v *Physic* (1826), it was ruled that a bill may be validly drawn up in pencil. It is not particularly common, but possible, for a bill to take up more than one page, as long as it is a single instrument (*KHR Financings Ltd* v *Jackson* (1977)). Another point is that the bill does not need to be written in the English language (*Arab Bank* v *Ross* (1952)).

Addressed by one person to another

Thirdly, the order must be addressed by one person to another. The import of that requirement is that the order must be addressed by the drawer to the drawee. By virtue of s 6(2) of the 1882 Act, there is scope for there to be more than two drawees.

Signed by the person giving it

Fourthly, the bill must be signed by the person giving it, ie it must be signed by the drawer. The common practice is for the drawer to sign the bill in its bottom right hand corner, but this is not an absolute requirement. Section 18(1) of the 1882 Act stipulates that a bill may be accepted by the drawee before it has been signed by the drawer or while it is otherwise incomplete. However, there is nothing in s 18(1) of the 1882 Act which compels a drawee to accept liability on a bill which has not been signed by the drawer (*McCall* v *Taylor* (1865)). By virtue of s 23(1) of the 1882 Act, it is provided that no person is liable as drawer, indorser, or acceptor of a bill who has not signed it as such. However, there are two exceptions. First, where a person signs a bill in a trade or assumed name, he is liable thereon as if he had signed it in his own name. Secondly, the signature of the name of a firm is equivalent to the signature by the person so signing of the names of all persons liable as partners in that firm. Moreover, in terms of s 24 of the 1882 Act, a forged signature on a bill is deemed to be wholly inoperative unless the party whose signature it purports to be has given his authority. Finally, s 91(1) of the 1882 Act is to the effect that it is not necessary that a person should sign it with his own hand, but that it is sufficient if his signature is written by some other person by or under his authority, eg an agent.

Payable on demand

Fifthly, the bill must be payable on demand or at a fixed or determinable future time. In terms of s 10(1) of the 1882 Act, if no time for payment is expressed on the bill, it is deemed to be payable on demand. Moreover, that section also directs that a bill is deemed to be payable on demand if it states that it is payable on sight or on presentation. If it is accepted or indorsed when it is overdue, it is deemed to be a bill payable on demand. Payment may also be in the future provided that the future event is certain to happen, eg on the death of the drawer, which will be valid (see *Roffey* v *Green* (1839)). However, if it is uncertain that the event will occur, then the bill will not be valid in terms of s 11 of the 1882 Act.

A sum certain in money

Sixthly, the sum payable must amount to a sum certain in money. Section 9(1) provides further guidance, directing that payments may be made in instalments. It is also acceptable that the bill provides for the payment of interest in terms of s 9(1) of the 1882 Act. If the rate of interest is unspecified, in English law, the bill is treated as valid in terms of the case of *Re Tillman* (1918) and 5% is deemed to be the appropriate rate, but there is Scottish authority in *Lamberton* v *Aiken* (1899) to the effect that such a bill would be invalid. In accordance with s 9 of the 1882 Act, interest is deemed to run from the date of the bill, or, if the bill is undated, from the issue thereof.

Made to the order of a specified person or to bearer

Seventhly, the bill must be made to the order of a specified person with reasonable certainty or to the bearer in terms of s 7(1) of the 1882 Act (see *Adam Associates (Strathclyde) Ltd* v *CGU Insurance plc* (2001)). The bill may be made payable to more than one person jointly or in the alternative. It may also be expressed to be payable to a person holding a particular office and if the specified person does not exist or is fictitious the bill is treated as being payable to the bearer (see *Clutton & Co* v *Attenborough & Son* (1897)).

The two categories of bill of exchange

It is implicit in the definition above in s 3(1) of the 1882 Act that there are two forms of bill of exchange: first, the specified payee bill, where a particular person is named as the person entitled to payment from the drawee on the bill, be it the original payee or a subsequent indorsee; and, secondly, the bearer bill, where the holder of the bill is entitled to payment, whomsoever that person may be. As expressed above, a specified payee bill and/or a bearer bill may be transferred by negotiation. In terms of s 31(2) of the 1882 Act, a bearer bill is negotiated by delivery only. In the case of a specified payee bill, s 31(3) of the 1882 Act provides that negotiation is conducted by indorsement and delivery whereby the payee or indorsee indorses the bill and delivers it over to a subsequent indorsee in return for payment. Hence, there is a crucial difference in the method of negotiation, depending on whether the bill is payable to the bearer or is payable to a specified payee. However, in each case, delivery of the bill is crucial: s 21(1) of the 1882 Act. Hence, although A may draw up a bill in favour of B, he is not liable on it until it is delivered to B. Likewise, if B indorses the bill to C, he will not be liable to C until it is delivered to C.

Indorsement: specified payee bill

In the context of a specified payee bill, s 33 of the 1882 Act regulates how indorsement must take place. First, an indorsement must be written on the bill itself and be signed by the indorser and the simple signature of the indorser on the bill, without additional words, is sufficient. The entire value of the bill must be indorsed and so the indorsement of only part of the amount payable on the face of the bill, or which purports to transfer the bill to two or more indorsees severally, does not operate to negotiate the bill. Where the payee or indorsee is wrongly designated on the bill or his name is spelt wrongly, that person may indorse the bill as described on the bill and add his proper signature. Where a person indorses a bill, s 55(2) of the 1882 Act directs that that person becomes conditionally liable to subsequent indorsees or payees in the event that the bill is dishonoured. However, that person may avoid liability by writing "without recourse" alongside his signature.

The "holder" of a bill

Only holders of a bill may negotiate it. Section 2 of the 1882 Act directs that a holder means the payee or indorsee of a bill who is possessor of it or the bearer of the bill (in the case of a bearer bill). The 1882 Act recognises two holders and there is a presumption that every holder is a "holder in due course" by virtue of s 30(2) of the 1882 Act.

Holder for value

A "holder for value" is someone who at any time has given value for the bill and that person is deemed to be a holder for value as regards the acceptor and all persons who became parties to the bill prior to value being given. A holder for value has certain rights under the 1882 Act and can enforce the bill against such persons, but the "holder in due course" has the full panoply of rights available under the 1882 Act.

Holder in due course

A "holder in due course" is a person who (1) has taken a bill complete and regular on the face of it, (2) became the holder of the bill before it became due for payment and without notice of it being dishonoured in any way, (3) took the bill in good faith and for value, and (4) when the bill was negotiated to him, had no notice of any defect in the title of the person who negotiated it. Section 2 of the 1882 Act states that "value" means valuable consideration and, in terms of s 90 of the 1882 Act, a matter is done in "good faith" if it is in fact done honestly, whether it is done negligently or not. The case of *Jones* v *Gordon* (1877) is authority for the proposition that a person will not be in good faith where he has a suspicion that something is wrong but makes no enquiry for fear of what will be uncovered. The effect of being a holder in due course is spelt out in s 38(2) of the 1882 Act which provides that the holder in due course holds the bill free from any defect in title of prior parties, as well as from personal defences available to prior parties among themselves, and may enforce payment against all parties liable on the bill. Thus, the holder in due course may enforce the bill even where it has been stolen or prior transactions between indorsees have been subject to fraud (*Whistler* v *Forster* (1863)). Thus, it is the holder in due course, rather than the holder for value, who enjoys the full beneficial effects of negotiability.

Liability on a bill

Sections 53–58 of the 1882 Act govern who will be liable on a bill of exchange and in what order such liability will attach. Obviously, the person one might initially think would be liable on a bill is the drawee, since the bill is drawn as an order on the drawee to make payment to the payee or indorsee. However, a drawee will only be liable on a bill when he accepts liability on the bill; and, where he refuses to accept such liability, he may be liable directly to the drawer who drew up the bill (*Hopkinson* v *Forster* (1874)).

"Funds attached" rule

By virtue of s 53(2) of the 1882 Act, where the drawee of a bill has in his hands funds available for the payment of the sum on the bill, the bill operates as an assignment of the sum for which it is drawn in favour of the holder, from the time when the bill is presented to the drawee. The effect of this subsection is that, on the presentation of the bill, the holder has the right to be paid any sum standing to the credit of the drawer which is held by the drawee up to the amount of the bill. This is shown by the case of *British Linen Bank* v *Carruthers* (1883) where the holder of a cheque for £161 presented it to the bank for payment. The bank rejected the cheque on the basis that the customer (who, of course, was the drawer of the bill) only had £136 in his account with the bank. The customer/drawer went bankrupt and the trustee in bankruptcy appointed over the estate of the customer/drawer claimed the £136 in the customer's account from the bank. However, the holder of the cheque who had presented it to the bank claimed that the £136 belonged to him on the basis that s 53(2) of the 1882 Act operated to assign the funds of the drawer held by the drawee to him. The court agreed with the holder. However, it must be stressed that the "funds attached" rule in s 53(2) of the 1882 Act no longer applies to cheques (ie it applies to bills of exchange only) presented for payment by virtue of s 254(4) of the 1882 Act.

Liability and duties of the acceptor

Section 54 of the 1882 Act regulates the liability of the acceptor on a bill by providing that when the acceptor accepts a bill, he undertakes to pay it according to the tenor of his acceptance. Section 54(2) directs that the acceptor is precluded from denying to a holder in due course (1) the existence of the drawer, the genuineness of his signature and his capacity and authority to draw the bill, (2) in the case of a bill payable to drawer's order, the then capacity of the drawer to indorse, but not the genuineness or validity of his indorsement, and (3) the existence of the payee and his then capacity to indorse, but not the genuineness or validity of his indorsement. However, it should be recalled that an acceptor is permitted to refuse payment on the bill by virtue of the fact that an indorsement is a forgery.

Enforcement against persons other than drawee

If the drawee dishonours the bill, s 55(1) of the 1882 Act enables the holder to enforce it against the drawer. By drawing up a bill, a drawer undertakes that on due presentment it shall be accepted and paid according to its tenor, and that if it is dishonoured the drawer will compensate the holder or any indorser who is compelled to pay it. The drawer is also precluded from denying to a holder in due course the existence of the payee and his then capacity to indorse. The effect of s 55(1) is that a drawer will have (1) primary liability on a bill if it is dishonoured by the drawee and/or (2) secondary liability on a bill if it is accepted by the drawee but payment is not made to the holder.

Enforcement against indorser

Where neither the drawee nor the drawer accept liability on the bill, the holder will be entitled to seek payment from an indorser on the bill. By indorsing a bill, an indorser does three things. First, the indorser undertakes that on due presentment it shall be accepted and paid, and that if it is dishonoured he will compensate the holder or a subsequent indorser who is compelled to pay it. Secondly, the indorser is precluded from denying to a holder in due course the genuineness and regularity in all respects of the drawer's signature and all previous indorsements. Finally, the indorser is precluded from denying to his immediate or a subsequent indorsee that the bill was at the time of his indorsement a valid and subsisting bill, and that he had then a good title thereto.

Discharge

Where a bill is presented and honoured by the drawee, acceptor, drawer or indorser, the bill is said to be "discharged", ie paid and honoured. Discharge can be contrasted with "dishonour" which arises where the bill is presented but not honoured by the drawee, etc.

Method of enforcement

A bill may be enforced in a number of ways. Most bills of exchange will be payable by the drawee on demand. In such a case, a bill which is expressed to be payable on demand will be enforced on the sight of the drawee or on presentation to the drawee. The effect of s 10(1) of the 1882 Act is that a bill which states that it is payable on demand, on sight or on presentation is duly deemed to be payable on demand. Where a bill is not so expressed, then in terms of s 39 of the 1882 Act, the bill must be presented to the drawee for acceptance. In terms of s 39, a bill must be presented for acceptance in three circumstances. First, where a bill expressly stipulates that it must be presented for acceptance, it must be so presented – even in circumstances where the bill is expressed to be payable on demand. Secondly, a bill must be presented for acceptance where it is drawn payable elsewhere than the residence or place of business of the drawee. Thirdly, a bill must be presented for acceptance where it is drawn payable at a certain period after sight. In the latter case, presentment for acceptance plays the part of determining the date of maturity (ie the date of payment) of the bill and the bill must be presented or negotiated within a reasonable time.

Presentment

Section 41 provides various rules on the method for the presentment of bills. First, presentment must be made by or on behalf of the holder to the drawee or to some person authorised to accept or refuse acceptance on his behalf at a reasonable hour on a business day and before the bill is overdue. Secondly, where the drawee is dead, presentment may be made to his personal representative, ie his executor. Where the drawee is bankrupt, presentment may be made to him or to his trustee in sequestration.

Presentment excused

Section 41(2) of the 1882 Act provides for situations where presentment for acceptance is excused and a bill may be treated as dishonoured for acceptance. First, such presentment is not necessary where the drawee is dead or bankrupt, or is a fictitious person or a person not having capacity to contract by bill. Secondly, the same applies where such presentment cannot be effected after the exercise of reasonable diligence. Thirdly, presentment is excused where, although the presentment has been irregular, acceptance has been refused on some other ground. Nevertheless, in terms of s 41(3) of the 1882 Act, the fact that the holder has reason to believe that the bill, on presentment, will be dishonoured does not excuse presentment.

Non-acceptance

Sections 42 and 43 of the 1882 Act govern the situation where a bill which must be presented for acceptance is not accepted by the parties stipulated in s 41. Sections 42 and 43 provide that "non-acceptance" is deemed to have occurred where a bill is presented for acceptance but is not accepted (ie acceptance is refused or cannot be obtained, or the bill is excused from presentment or acceptance and is not accepted) within the customary time. At that point, the holder must treat it as dishonoured, and, if the holder fails to treat it so, he loses his right of recourse against the drawer and the indorsers. If the holder does so treat the bill as dishonoured for non-acceptance, he enjoys a right of recourse against the drawer and indorsers and no presentment for payment is required.

Presentment for payment

Once the bill has been presented for acceptance, the holder must present the bill for payment, unless presentment for payment is excused. If the bill is not presented for payment, the drawer and indorser are released from liability in terms of s 45 of the 1882 Act. Where the bill is dishonoured and a notice of dishonour is given to the drawer and each indorser in accordance with s 48 of the 1882 Act, the holder is entitled to claim damages.

Essential Facts

- A bill of exchange is an unconditional order in writing, addressed by one person to another, signed by the person giving it, requiring the person to whom it is addressed to pay on demand, or at a fixed or determinable future time, a sum certain in money to or to the order of a specified person, or to the bearer.
- A bill of exchange may be a specified payee bill or a bearer bill.
- The relevant parties to a bill of exchange are the drawer, drawee, payee, indorsee and holder.
- A holder of a bill may be a "holder for value" or a "holder in due course".

Essential Cases

Connal & Co v Loder (1868): in the case of transfer by negotiation, there is no requirement for (1) intimation of the transfer of the debt to the account debtor or (2) a separate document of transfer.

Hamilton v Spottiswoode (1849): the words "we hereby authorise you to pay" on a document were insufficient to constitute an "unconditional order".

Geary v Physic (1826): a bill may be validly drawn up in pencil.

KHR Financings Ltd v Jackson (1977): a bill may take up more than one page, as long as it is a single instrument.

Arab Bank v Ross (1952): a bill does not need to be written in the English language.

Roffey v Green (1839): a bill may provide for payment in the future provided that the future event is certain to happen, eg on the death of the drawer.

Clutton & Co v Attenborough & Son (1897): a bill will be valid where it is expressed to be payable to a person holding a particular office, or, if the specified person does not exist or is fictitious, the bill is treated as being payable to the bearer.

Hopkinson v Forster (1874): a drawee will only be liable on a bill when he accepts liability on the bill; and, where he refuses to accept such liability, he may be liable directly to the drawer who drew up the bill.

British Linen Bank v Carruthers (1883): authority for the "funds attached" rule which applies to bills of exchange in terms of s 53(2) of the 1882 Act.

8 CONSUMER CREDIT

FORMS OF CONSUMER CREDIT

The Consumer Credit Act 1974 ("the Act") governs the regulation of various forms of credit made available to consumers. Credit may be provided in a number of guises.

Lender credit

The most straightforward kind of credit is lender credit. Here, a lender advances credit facilities to a customer in return for the customer repaying the credit over a definite or indefinite period of time in standard payments, together with fixed or variable interest rates. Term loan facilities and overdraft facilities advanced by financial institutions, banks and building societies fall into this "lender credit" category. Lender credit may be secured over the assets of the customer (eg a standard security) or it may be unsecured.

Vendor credit

The other form of credit regulated by the Act is "vendor credit". Here, the vendor of goods extends credit to a buyer in relation to the sale of its goods to the buyer. The best-known form of "vendor credit" is hire purchase. Here, the seller of goods transfers possession of the goods to the debtor – but title to the goods does not pass to the debtor. A hire-purchase contract is not a contract of sale and so the Sale of Goods Act 1979 does not apply to the former kind of contract (*Helby* v *Matthews* (1895)). A hire-purchase agreement is entered into between the seller and the debtor whereby the seller hires the goods to the debtor in return for the debtor making regular payments to the seller. At the end of the duration of the hire payments, the agreement confers an option – but not an obligation – in favour of the debtor to purchase the goods on the transfer of a final nominal payment to the seller. Hire purchase can be contrasted with a contract of hire by virtue of the fact that in the latter there is no option or intention to transfer title to the goods to the buyer/debtor.

Credit sale and conditional sale agreements

Another form of vendor credit is the credit sale agreement. Here, title to the goods passes immediately from the seller to the buyer/debtor. The buyer/debtor then makes payments to the seller in instalments. This can be contrasted with a conditional sale agreement. This kind of contract is different since title only passes to the buyer on the payment of the final instalment. Conditional sale agreements resemble hire-purchase agreements. However, the distinguishing factor is that title passes to the buyer automatically on the payment of the final instalment in the case of a conditional sale agreement, whereas, in the case of hire purchase, payment of the final instalment simply confers an option on the debtor to purchase the goods, ie a sale is not certain. The crucial point is that hire purchase does not involve a sale. However, credit sale and conditional sale agreements are, by definition, sales.

Credit cards

Credit cards are also regulated by the Act. The majority of credit cards permit customers to use the card up to a pre-arranged credit limit. When the customer presents his credit card to a seller/merchant, the seller/merchant is entitled to, and claims, payment from the credit card company. The customer is then liable to pay the credit card company the sum remitted to the seller/merchant pursuant to the sale transaction. The legal characteristics of a credit card arrangement were analysed in detail by the Court of Appeal in *Re Charge Card Services (No 2)* (1989). The court explained that a credit card transaction was made up of three separate contracts, as follows:

- a contract between the credit card company and the seller/merchant in terms of which the credit card company agrees to pay the seller/ merchant in respect of the goods or services acquired by the customer and the seller/merchant agrees to accept payment from the credit card company;
- a contract between the credit card company and the customer in terms of which the customer is issued with a credit card which empowers them to purchase goods or services from sellers/merchants and the customer agrees to make payment for those goods or services to the credit card company together with interest; and
- A contract between the customer and the seller/merchant in terms of which (a) the latter agrees to sell goods or supply services to the former and (b) the latter agrees to accept payment for the goods or services via a credit card in substitution for payment by cash.

Thus, in a credit card arrangement, the seller/merchant agrees to accept the credit card company's obligation to pay as opposed to the customer assuming an obligation to pay the seller/merchant directly. Hence, if the customer tenders payment by credit card, his liability to the seller/merchant to make payment for the goods is immediately discharged.

CONSUMER CREDIT LICENCES

The Act introduces a system whereby certain persons providing credit to consumers must first obtain a licence. The purpose of the licensing system is to protect consumers. In terms of s 21(1) of the Act, a person must obtain a consumer credit licence where they carry on a "consumer credit business", a "consumer hire business" or an "ancillary credit business". Section 189(1) of the Act defines a "consumer credit business" as any business being carried on by a person so far as it comprises or relates to the provision of credit by him or otherwise his being a creditor under a regulated consumer credit agreement. Under s 189(1) of the Act, a "consumer hire business" is defined as any business being carried on by a person so far as it comprises or relates to the hiring of goods by him, or otherwise his being an owner under a regulated consumer hire agreement.

A person is not to be treated as carrying on a particular type of business merely because occasionally he enters into transactions belonging to a business of that type. Therefore, in terms of s 189(2) of the Act, the main and regular activity of a person must be one of the above three businesses for them to require to apply for a licence. A good example is provided by *Hare* v *Schurek* (1993).

Types of licence

Section 22(1) of the Act provides for two licences: a standard licence; and a group licence. Most traders will require a standard licence. An application for a standard licence will be granted by the OFT in terms of s 25 of the Act if it is satisfied that the applicant is a "fit and proper person" to carry on the type of business applied for. Meanwhile group licences will be required by groups of traders (not companies in a corporate group) in circumstances in which it is unnecessary in the public interest to require them individually to apply for a standard licence.

REGULATED AGREEMENTS

The Act provides for the regulation of the provision of credit as well as the supervision of the credit industry in terms of the licensing system.

The regulatory reach of the Act extends to consumer credit agreements, consumer hire agreements and exempt agreements (exempt agreements are those entered into by "high net worth" individuals in terms of s 16A of the Act and the Consumer Credit (Exempt Agreements) Order 2007 (SI 2007/1168) or by a debtor for the purposes of a business under s 16B of the Act) entered into by individuals – which are referred to generically as "regulated agreements". An "individual" is defined in s 189(1) of the Act as an actual human being, a partnership consisting of two or three persons not all of whom are bodies corporate and an unincorporated body of persons which does not consist entirely of bodies corporate and is not a partnership. However, s 16B of the Act stipulates that the Act does not regulate consumer credit agreements by which the creditor provides the debtor with credit in excess of £25,000 or a consumer hire agreement that requires the hirer to make payments in excess of £25,000 if the agreement is made wholly or predominantly for the purposes of a business carried on or intended to be carried on by him. Thus, the effect of these provisions is that the Act does not extend to regulated agreements which are entered into for business purposes if the credit sum exceeds £25,000.

Consumer credit agreement

Section 8(1) of the Act provides that a consumer credit agreement is an agreement in terms of which the creditor gives the debtor credit of any amount. The definition of "credit" in s 9(1) of the Act is particularly wide to the effect that it covers a loan or any other form of financial accommodation. Thus, it is sufficiently broad to include hire-purchase contracts, conditional sale contracts and credit sale contracts. In calculating the amount of credit, s 9(4) directs that the total charge for credit is excluded. The total charge for credit is defined by ss 20 and 189 of the Act and the Consumer Credit (Total Charge for Credit) Regulations 1980 (SI 1980/51) and includes the interest charged, security transaction costs and credit brokerage costs.

Types of consumer credit agreement

Consumer credit agreements are classified based on their purposes rather than the legal forms which they take. The most significant are:

- *fixed sum credit* – s 10(1)(b) of the Act states that this is a form of credit where the sum does not vary, eg a loan or hire-purchase agreement;

- *running account credit* – in terms of s 10(1)(a) of the Act, such credit is of the type where the debtor has the right to obtain cash, goods or services from the creditor from time to time, eg a store card, credit card or overdraft;

- *restricted use credit* – s 11(1) of the Act provides that such credit is used to finance a specific transaction between the debtor and creditor or supplier, eg a hire-purchase agreement;

- *unrestricted use credit* – this enables the debtor to use credit as he wishes in terms of s 11(2) of the Act, eg an overdraft;

- *debtor-creditor agreements* – by virtue of s 13 of the Act, this is an agreement between a debtor and creditor for the extension of credit without the supplier of the goods or services being involved in the arrangement at all;

- *debtor-creditor-supplier agreements* – such contracts may involve two parties, (eg a debtor and supplier where the supplier sells goods and extends credit to the debtor to enable them to purchase the goods) or three parties, namely a debtor, creditor and supplier (eg a credit card).

A consumer credit agreement must either be a debtor-creditor agreement or a debtor-creditor-supplier agreement.

Consumer hire agreement

Section 15 directs that a consumer hire agreement is an agreement to hire goods entered into by an individual which is not a hire-purchase agreement and is capable of lasting for more than 3 months in duration. With regard to the latter criteria, the fact that either party has a contractual right at any time to terminate an agreement of indefinite duration does not deprive that agreement of the status of a consumer hire agreement.

CONTROLS ON ENTERING INTO AGREEMENTS

Pre-contractual information

Section 55 of the Act and the Consumer Credit (Disclosure of Information) Regulations 2004 (SI 2004/1481) enjoin creditors or owners to provide certain information to the debtor or hirer before a consumer credit or consumer hire agreement is formed. In terms of s 55(2) of the Act, the effect of a failure to perform such obligations means that the agreement is not properly executed and so a court order is required before the creditor can enforce the agreement.

First, s 56 regulates antecedent negotiations, ie any negotiations entered into between the debtor or hirer and (i) the creditor or owner, (ii) a credit broker who supplies the creditor with goods to be supplied to the debtor under a debtor-creditor-supplier agreement involving two parties or (iii) the supplier in a debtor-creditor-supplier agreement involving three parties. Section 56(4) states that negotiations commence when the debtor and the negotiator begin communications orally or by advertisement, including all dealings, dialogue or representations made by the negotiator to the debtor. The point of s 56(3) of the Act is that an agreement is void insofar as it attempts to negate the creditor's liability for the acts or omissions of the negotiator or make the negotiator the debtor's agent: see *UDT* v *Whitfield* (1987) and *Durkin* v *DSG Retail Ltd* (2008).

Control of content and form

Section 60 of the Act goes on to control the content and form of consumer credit and consumer hire agreements. Certain prescribed information must be contained in the agreements and such information must be given prominence, be distinguishable and easily legible. Moreover, information of a financial nature must be presented as a whole. The requisite content is governed by the Consumer Credit (Agreement) Regulations 1983 (SI 1983/1553) and includes the following:

- the names and addresses of the parties;
- a prominent heading on the first page detailing the legal nature of the agreement, eg that it is a hire-purchase agreement regulated under the Act;
- the cash price;
- details of any deposit paid or other advance payment;
- the amount of credit or credit limit;
- the annual percentage rate and how it is calculated;
- the total amount payable;
- the duration or minimum duration of the agreement;
- information regarding the timing and amount of payments;
- details of default charges;
- information regarding any security provided by the debtor or hirer;

- details of the rights, obligations and remedies in terms of the Act; and
- if the agreement cannot be cancelled, a statement to that effect.

The agreement must include all express terms in terms of s 61 of the Act and it must contain a signature box for the debtor or hirer. Section 61(1)(a) of the Act directs that the creditor or owner and the debtor or hirer must sign the agreement in proper form in the signature box. All of the above prescribed content must be included in the agreement. If it is not so included, the effect is that the Act will have been breached. Moreover, the agreement must be properly executed, since, if it is not, the effect of s 65(1) and (2) of the Act is that it cannot be enforced against the debtor or hirer (in terms of retaking possession of the goods) without the leave of the court. Sections 61–64 of the Act direct that in order to be properly executed the document capturing the agreement must be set out in prescribed form, contain all of its prescribed terms including all the terms of the agreement (except implied terms), be legible, be signed as prescribed by the parties and, if the agreement may be cancelled in terms of the Act, it must contain the information prescribed in s 64 of the Act concerning the cancellation rights and their exercise. Finally, all copies of the agreement require to be supplied to the debtor or hirer by the creditor, owner or negotiator in terms of ss 62 and 63 of the Act.

Delivery of copies of executed and unexecuted agreements

Sections 62 and 63 of the Act deal with the delivery of copies of un-executed and executed agreements to the debtor or hirer. In circumstances where the creditor or owner has signed the agreement before the debtor or hirer signs it, s 63(1) of the Act stipulates that a copy of the executed agreement, and of any other document referred to in it, must be there and then delivered to the debtor or hirer. However, if the agreement has not been signed by the creditor or owner when it is presented to the debtor or hirer for signature, then the debtor or hirer must be given a copy of the agreement on signing it together with a further copy of the executed agreement, and of any other document referred to in it, within 7 days of the creditor or owner signing it.

Right to withdraw

The Act provides the debtor or hirer with certain rights to withdraw from a consumer credit or consumer hire agreement. If the creditor or owner has not signed the agreement at the point in time when the debtor or hirer signs it, the debtor or hirer is entitled to withdraw from the prospective agreement at any time before the former signs. Section 57(2) and (3) of the Act regulates the manner of withdrawal to the effect that written or oral notice of withdrawal may be given by the creditor or owner and others. In terms of s 57(1) of the Act, the effect of a withdrawal is the same as a cancellation of the regulated agreement under s 69 of the Act.

Right of cancellation

The cancellation of regulated agreements is governed by s 67 of the Act and is intended to afford the debtor or hirer a period of reflection where the agreement has been signed away from the trade premises of the creditor, owner or negotiator. The debtor is entitled to cancel where oral representations are made by an individual acting as a negotiator (see above for a definition of who may constitute a negotiator) or someone on his behalf in the presence of the debtor or hirer in the course of antecedent negotiations where the agreement was signed by the debtor or hirer away from trade premises of the creditor, owner or negotiator. A representation is any statement of fact or opinion made before the contract is executed which is material to any of the matters being negotiated and capable of influencing the debtor's or hirer's judgement of whether or not to enter into the agreement or which is capable of inducing the debtor or hirer to enter into the agreement, whether or not the negotiator intended such statement to induce entry into the agreement (*Moorgate Services* v *Kabir* (1995)). Section 64(1) of the Act directs that in circumstances where an agreement is cancellable, every copy of the agreement must include a notice in the prescribed form indicating the right of the debtor or hirer to cancel, how and when that right may be exercised and to whom (including the address) that notice of cancellation may be sent.

The point in time at which the notice referred to above in terms of s 64(1)(b) of the Act or the second copy of the agreement is sent, dictates when the cooling-off period of 5 days referred to in s 68 of the Act ends. The effect of ss 69(1) and 68(1) of the Act is that a debtor or hirer may cancel a regulated agreement within the cooling-off period, which begins when the debtor or hirer signs the agreement and continues until 5 days after the date when the debtor or hirer receives the s 64(1)(b) notice or the second copy of the agreement. The notice must be in writing and must be sent to the creditor or owner or to someone specified in the s 64(1)(b) notice. It does not require to be in any particular form. However, it must indicate the intention of the debtor or hirer to withdraw from the agreement.

Consequences of cancellation

Section 69(1)(c) of the Act stipulates that the service of a notice of cancellation operates to cancel the agreement. Section 70(1) of the Act provides that any sums paid under the agreement are repayable by the creditor or owner to the debtor or hirer. Sums which are stated to be payable by the debtor or hirer under the agreement cease to be so payable but sums paid by the creditor or owner to a supplier on behalf of the debtor or hirer under a debtor-creditor-supplier agreement become repayable to the creditor. The effect of s 72(4) of the Act is that all other goods held by the debtor or hirer must be returned to the creditor or owner.

MATTERS ARISING DURING THE CURRENCY OF THE AGREEMENT

Provision of information

Sections 77, 77A, 78, 79 and 80 of the Act provide for the provision of information on request and statements automatically to the debtor or hirer in the case of a fixed-sum creditor agreement, running account credit agreement or consumer hire agreement. On request, during the course of a regulated agreement, a debtor or hirer may request a copy of the agreement and a statement of the account between them from the creditor. Sections 77, 78 and 79 of the Act direct that the statement in the case of a fixed-sum creditor agreement, running account credit agreement and/or a consumer hire agreement, must include a note of the sums paid to date by the debtor, sums remaining unpaid and the remaining total sums to be paid. The creditor has 12 days to respond to such requests, failing which he will not be entitled to enforce the agreement so long as he continues to remain in default.

Implied terms

A consumer credit or consumer hire agreement will be comprised of particular express and implied terms. The implied terms included within a hire-purchase agreement are statutory in origin and found in ss 8–11 of the Supply of Goods (Implied Terms) Act 1973 ("the 1973 Act"). These implied terms mirror those contained in ss 12–15 of the Sale of

Goods Act 1979. For example, s 8 of the 1973 Act provides that there is an implied term on the part of the creditor that he will have a right to sell the goods at the time when property is to pass, that the goods are free and will remain free from any charges or encumbrances at the time when property in the goods is to pass and that the hirer will enjoy quiet possession of the goods. Moreover, in terms of s 9 of the 1973 Act, there is an implied term that goods hired will conform to their description. Section 10 of the 1973 Act goes on to stipulate that goods hired must be of satisfactory quality and reasonably fit for purpose and s 11 states that goods sold must conform to sample. Likewise, ss 7–10 of the Supply of Goods and Services Act 1982 provide that the same implied terms apply in the case of contracts of hire.

Section 75 connected lender liability

The concept of connected lender liability is found in s 75 of the Act and implicit within it is a recognition that trade sellers and finance companies usually have a close relationship. The basic premise of s 75 of the Act is that breaches of a contract of sale by a trade seller will have implications for the creditor in terms of the back-to-back consumer credit or consumer hire agreement. It directs that if a debtor under a debtor-creditor-supplier agreement involving three parties has, in relation to a transaction financed by the agreement, any claim against the supplier in respect of a misrepresentation or breach of contract, he shall have a like claim against the creditor, who will be jointly and severally liable to the debtor alongside the supplier. So if the supplier is liable to the debtor for breach of contract or misrepresentation, the creditor will also be liable. This provision is particularly useful for, and protective of, consumers in a credit card transaction.

In the case of *OFT* v *Lloyds TSB Bank plc* (2007), the Court of Appeal held that s 75 also applies to credit card transactions involving a fourth party merchant acquirer. Moreover, in *OFT* v *Lloyds TSB Bank plc* (2007), the House of Lords ruled that s 75 also applied to purchases made abroad by debtors from suppliers with a credit card. However, s 187(3A) of the Act specifically directs that s 75 of the Act does not apply to debit cards.

TERMINATION AND DEFAULT OF REGULATED AGREEMENTS

Section 94 of the Act stipulates that a debtor is entitled at any time to terminate a regulated agreement by providing written notice to the creditor and making payment to the creditor of all amounts due. The notice may embody the exercise by the debtor of any option to purchase goods conferred on him by the agreement, and deal with any other matter arising on, or in relation to, the termination of the agreement. Section 95 of the Act states that the debtor will have the right to a rebate on the charge for credit which is calculated in accordance with the rules set out in the Consumer Credit (Rebate on Early Settlement) Regulations 1983 (SI 1983/1562).

Termination of consumer hire agreements by hirer

Section 101(1) and (3) of the Act deals specifically with consumer hire agreements. Notwithstanding the fact that a consumer hire agreement may be of an indefinite duration, it is provided that the hirer is entitled to terminate the agreement by giving notice to the owner or any person entitled or authorised to receive the sums payable under the agreement where that agreement has endured for a period of at least 18 months. In terms of s 101(4) and (5) of the Act, the period in respect of which the hirer is obliged to give notice to the creditor represents the shorter of 3 months and the period between hire payments. However, there are certain circumstances where termination of a consumer hire agreement is excluded in terms of s 101(7) of the Act as follows:

- where the agreement provides for payment which in total exceeds £1,500 pa;
- where the goods are hired by the hirer for business purposes and the goods are selected by the hirer, which are then acquired by the owner from a third party at his request; or
- where, in terms of the agreement, the hirer requires the goods for the purposes of hiring them to third parties in the course of a business.

Termination of hire-purchase and conditional sale agreements by debtor or hirer

Section 99(1) of the Act provides that a debtor or hirer under a hire-purchase agreement or conditional sale agreement is entitled to terminate it and return the goods at any time before the final payment falls due in terms of the agreement by providing notice to persons authorised to receive payments in terms of the agreement. By virtue of s 99(2) of the Act, the termination of such an agreement does not affect any liability under the agreement which has accrued before the termination, ie the debtor or hirer is not relieved of any liability for payments due before termination. However, s 101(1) of the Act directs that the debtor must pay the creditor up to half the total price in terms of the agreement if the debtor takes advantage of the s 99 right to terminate early. If the court is satisfied that a sum less than that amount would be equal to the loss sustained by the creditor in consequence of the termination of the agreement by the debtor, the court may make an order for the payment of that sum in lieu of that amount. Thus, on the face of it, ss 99 and 100 are useful for a debtor who is struggling to make payments in terms of the regulated agreement. Nevertheless, in practice, regulated agreements will commonly contain an accelerated payments clause which stipulates that the debtor is obliged to make all payments under the agreement in the event that the debtor defaults on any payment, ie all payments become due and payable. In the case of *Wadham Stringer Finance Ltd* v *Meaney* (1981), it was held that such an accelerated payments clause will not be a common law penalty where the creditor affords the debtor a rebate for early settlement. In terms of s 87(1) of the Act, the creditor must serve a default notice on the debtor before such an accelerated payments clause can have immediate effect.

Creditor's right to repossess goods in the case of hire-purchase and conditional sale agreements

In circumstances where the debtor defaults without seeking to terminate a hire-purchase or conditional sale agreement, the creditor will look to repossess the goods hired. In terms of s 90(1) of the Act, where the debtor has paid a reasonable amount of instalments for the goods, namely one-third of the total price or more, the creditor must first obtain an order from the court to repossess the goods "from the debtor". Section 90(7) of the Act refers to the goods as "protected goods". The consequences of a breach of s 90 by the creditor are outlined in s 91 of the Act to the effect that the agreement, if not previously terminated, shall terminate and the debtor is released from all liability under the agreement and has the right to recover all sums already paid (but the creditor may retake possession of the goods without breaching s 90 if:

- the debtor has transferred the goods to a third party (but if the debtor has left the goods with a third party by way of loan, the creditor will not be able to take advantage of s 90 by virtue of the decision in *Bentinck* v *Cromwell Engineering Ltd* (1971));
- the debtor has abandoned the goods; or
- the debtor permits the creditor to repossess the goods – (see *Mercantile Credit Co* v *Cross* (1965)).

Provision of information to debtors and hirers

Debtors who are struggling to meet their payments under a regulated agreement are entitled to various items of information. First, by virtue of s 86B of the Act, the creditor must serve a notice of arrears upon the debtor in prescribed form (in terms of the Consumer Credit (Information Requirements and Duration of Licences and Charges) Regulations 2007 (SI 2007/1167)) in circumstances where the debtor has entered into a consumer hire agreement or fixed-sum agreement and has fallen two payments behind. That notice must be served within 14 days of the debtor falling two payments behind.

Secondly, the provisions of ss 86E and 187A of the Act stipulate that the creditor must serve a default sum notice on the debtor where the debtor is due to pay a default sum under the agreement as a result of breach. The notice of such default sums must be served within the prescribed period after the default sum becomes payable according to s 86E(2) of the Act. In accordance with s 86E(5) of the Act, if the creditor or owner fails to serve the default sum notice upon the debtor or hirer within the prescribed period mentioned, he shall not be entitled to enforce the agreement until the notice is given to the debtor or hirer.

Thirdly, according to s 86A of the Act, the OFT is entrusted with the preparation of an arrears information sheet and a default information sheet. The purpose of these information sheets is to provide debtors and hirers with assistance so that they are aware of the effects of notices of arrears and/or default sum notices which may have been served upon them by the creditor or owner in terms of ss 86B and/or 86C of the Act. The creditor and owner are under a duty to send such sheets to debtors or hirers when they send notices of arrears or default sum notices.

Default notices

Where the debtor is in breach of a regulated agreement, the creditor or owner must first serve a default notice upon the debtor or hirer before they may enforce their rights under the agreement. Section 88(1) of the Act states that the creditor is prevented from securing each of the following enforcement remedies listed in s 87 unless he has first served such a default notice in the prescribed form (in terms of the Consumer Credit (Enforcement, Default and Termination Notices) Regulations 1993 (SI 1993/1561)) upon the debtor:

- the right to demand early payment of any sum, eg in terms of a contractually agreed accelerated payments clause;

- the right to terminate the agreement;
- the right to recover possession of the goods sold or hired; or
- the treatment of any of the debtor's rights as terminated, deferred or restricted.

There is no requirement for a creditor to serve a default notice upon a debtor in order to sue for sums which are already due and payable under the agreement.

Content and form of default notices

The content of the notice is governed by s 88(1) as follows:

- it must contain details of the breach;
- it must outline what must be done in order to remedy the breach in the event that it is remediable;
- it must set out what sum is required to be paid as compensation for the breach in the case of an irremediable breach, together with a notice of the date before which it is to be paid; and
- it must contain a statement regarding the implications of a failure on the part of the debtor to remedy the defect or pay the sum.

The period permitted for payment must be at least 14 days from the date of the service of the notice upon the debtor. A default notice will be invalid where the sum due is overstated to a significant degree in the default notice (*Woodchester Lease Management Services Ltd* v *Swain* (1999)).

Where the debtor complies with the default notice, eg by making payment within the stipulated 14 days, s 89 of the Act states that the breach will be treated as if it had never occurred. However, a failure on the part of the debtor to take the requisite action in terms of the default notice within the 14-day period entitles the creditor to take the enforcement remedies under s 87 of the Act (see above). Finally, in terms of ss 76 and 98 of the Act, the creditor must give the debtor a separate notice called a non-default notice before it exercises a right to do any of the following in circumstances where (1) that right is given to the creditor in terms of the agreement and (2) the debtor is not in breach of the agreement:

- the right to demand the early payment of any sum, eg in terms of a contractually agreed accelerated payments clause;
- the right to terminate the agreement; or
- the right to recover possession of the goods sold or hired.

This provision is applicable in situations where a clause of the agreement enables the creditor to do any of the above on the occurrence of a certain event which in itself does not amount to a breach of contract (eg the insolvency of the debtor).

JUDICIAL CONTROL

The Act sets out a range of orders which may be granted by the court in relation to the control of consumer credit and consumer hire agreements. In prescribing such orders, the court also has a range of powers. For example, in terms of s 135 of the Act, the court has the power to make one of its orders duly conditional on the doing of some act or acts by any party to the proceedings. By virtue of s 136 of the Act, the court may in any order made by it, include such provision as it considers just for amending any agreement or security in consequence of a term of the order.

The range of court orders

Where an agreement has been improperly executed, the terms of s 127 of the Act are such that a creditor must first obtain an enforcement order in advance of enforcing the agreement. Alternatively, the court may grant a time order. The objective of a time order (set out in s 129 of the Act) is to give the debtor extra time to pay. Such time orders may be sought by a debtor. The court may also grant a return and transfer order in terms of s 133 of the Act where the agreement is a hire-purchase agreement or conditional sale agreement. In terms of a return order, the creditor is entitled to the return of the goods. Section 131 of the Act stipulates that a protection order is available on the application of a creditor or owner. It protects the property of the creditor or owner from damage or depreciation pending the outcome of any proceedings which have been initiated under the Act. Furthermore, where the court forms the view that the relationship established between the debtor and creditor in terms of a credit agreement is unfair to the debtor, the court has the power to make a number of orders in terms of s 140B of the Act. Such orders are of the nature that the court has a wide power to revise a credit agreement if it is minded to do so. Finally, the court may make an order under s 132 of the Act which provides financial relief to hirers in circumstances where the owner of the goods recovers them by virtue of, or without, taking court action.

Essential Facts

- The Consumer Credit Act 1974 ("the Act") regulates lender credit, vendor credit, credit sale agreements, conditional sale agreements and credit cards.
- Persons providing credit to consumers in the course of a consumer credit business must first obtain a consumer credit licence.
- Consumer credit agreements and consumer hire agreements are regulated by the Act.
- Pre-contractual information and the form and content of consumer credit agreements and consumer hire agreements are controlled by the Act.
- The Act provides a debtor with a right to withdraw and cancel a regulated agreement.
- Section 75 of the Act provides for connected lender liability whereby breaches of a contract of sale by a trade seller will have implications for the creditor in terms of the back-to-back consumer credit or consumer hire agreement.
- The Act places controls on the termination of consumer hire agreements by the hirer and the termination of hire-purchase and conditional sale agreements by the debtor or hirer.
- Where the debtor is in breach of a regulated agreement, the creditor or owner must first serve a default notice upon the debtor or hirer before they may enforce their rights under the agreement.
- The courts are provided with the right to make a range of orders which control the content and exercise of rights of creditors under regulated agreements.

Essential Cases

Helby v Matthews (1895): a hire-purchase contract is not a contract of sale and so the Sale of Goods Act 1979 does not apply to the former kind of contract.

Re Charge Card Services (No 2) (1989): a credit card transaction comprises three separate contracts.

Hare v Schurek (1993): a businessman not in the habit of providing credit to his customers did not require a consumer credit licence when he entered into a hire-purchase agreement with a finance company and supplied the motor car to a customer on financial terms which mirrored his liabilities to the finance company.

Moorgate Services v Kabir (1995): a representation is a statement of fact or opinion made before the contract is executed which is material to any of the matters being negotiated and capable of inducing the debtor or hirer to enter into the agreement or influencing the debtor's or hirer's judgement of whether or not to enter into the agreement.

OFT v Lloyds TSB Bank plc (2007): the Court of Appeal held that s 75 of the Act applied to credit card transactions involving a fourth party merchant acquirer.

OFT v Lloyds TSB Bank plc (2007): the House of Lords ruled that s 75 of the Act also applied to purchases made abroad by debtors from suppliers with a credit card.

Wadham Stringer Finance Ltd v Meaney (1981): an accelerated payments clause will not be a common law penalty where the creditor affords the debtor a rebate for early settlement.

Bentinck v Cromwell Engineering Ltd (1971): where the debtor has left the goods with a third party by way of loan, the creditor will not be able to take advantage of s 90 of the Act to repossess the goods without first obtaining a court order.

9 INTELLECTUAL PROPERTY

Many businesses own valuable assets which are intangible and represent the culmination of years of research and development. For example, a company may create a new method of doing something such as an invention or create a logo which differentiates that company or that company's products from its competitors. The company might be in the business of entertainment whereupon its songs, plays or written works attract great popular appeal. In such circumstances, the area of commercial law known as intellectual property assumes great importance. Intellectual property law establishes rules and procedures whereby such innovations or productions may be created, legally recognised and protected. In this chapter, we will consider the main types of intellectual property right which are recognised by the law, namely copyright, patents, trade marks and designs.

COPYRIGHT

Introduction

The law of copyright is governed by the Copyright, Designs and Patents Act 1988 ("CDPA"). In terms of ss 1–8 of CDPA, copyright may exist in literary, dramatic, musical or artistic works, films, broadcasts, sound recordings and typographical arrangements of published works. It is provided in s 3(1) of CDPA that a table or compilation, a computer program, the preparatory design material for a computer program and a database are all examples of a literary work. Dramatic works include works of dance or mime and a musical work means a work consisting of music, exclusive of any words or action intended to be sung, spoken or performed with the music.

Originality

There is a requirement that the literary, dramatic, musical or artistic work be "original" and "recorded, in writing or otherwise" in terms of ss 1(1)(a) and s 3(2) of CDPA. The threshold for demonstrating originality is not particularly onerous. The *dictum* of Peterson J in the case of *University of London Press Ltd* v *University Tutorial Press Ltd* (1916) is to the effect that the work does not require to be representative of the expression of original or inventive thought. It is enough that the originality relates to the expression of some thought. That requirement will be satisfied if the work has not been copied from another work and so has originated from the author. In *University of London Press*, it was held that exam papers would attract copyright protection.

The requirement for originality is complemented by the need for some expenditure of effort, skill and labour by the author in the case of a compilation work, ie a work which adapts, organises or arranges an existing work or works. Moreover, the effect of the rule that the work must be recorded is that the law does not recognise copyright in ideas, only ideas which have been expressed or articulated. Sections 153–155 of CDPA also stipulate that there must be a sufficiently close connection between the UK and the author of the work, the place where it was first published or the place from which it was first made (if the work is one of broadcast).

Authorship

Section 9 of CDPA defines the author as the person who creates the work, or the producer in the case of a sound recording, the producer and director in the case of a film, the person making the broadcast in the case of a broadcast, and the publisher in the case of the typographical arrangement of a published edition. The effect of being an author is delimited in s 11(1) of CDPA to the effect that the author is deemed to be the first owner of any copyright in it. However, there are exceptions: eg where an employee makes the work *in the course of his employment*, his employer is the first owner of any copyright in the work subject to any agreement to the contrary. In the case of a literary, dramatic, musical or artistic work, the copyright endures for 70 years from the end of the calendar year in which the author dies, whereupon it expires, by virtue of s 12(2) of CDPA. A distinction should be made between the author and the owner and it ought to be emphasised that the author is relevant for the purposes of the 70-year rule, even in circumstances where the ownership of the copyright has been transferred. In the case of a film, s 13B(2) of CDPA directs that the copyright expires at the end of the period of 70 years from the end of the calendar year in which the death occurs of the last to die of the principal director, the author of the screenplay, the author of the dialogue, or the composer of music specially created for and used in the film. As for sound recordings, in terms of the provisions of s 13B(2) of CDPA, copyright in the sound recording expires at the end of the period of 50 years from the end of the calendar year in which the recording is made, or, if during that period the recording is published, 50 years from the end of the calendar year in which it is first published, or, if during that period the recording is not published but is released to the public by being played in public or communicated to the public, 50 years from the end of the calendar year in which it is first so made available.

The two components of copyright

The right of copyright is comprised of two components. First, there is the economic right which attaches to the copyright work. This enables the owner to exploit the work for financial reward, eg by being paid every time that the work is published, played, transmitted, shown, etc. It also confers upon the owner the right to prevent unlicensed reproduction and dealings in the work. It is the economic right that is essentially a property right: ie since the owner owns the copyright, he may alienate it, license it, grant security over it, in return for a loan, etc. This can be contrasted with moral rights. Moral rights recognise interests of the author other than economic rights, and are continuing in nature.

Moral rights

An author will have moral rights even in circumstances where he has assigned his ownership of the copyright or the physical form of the work first recorded. First, where the author has asserted his moral rights in accordance with s 78 of CDPA, s 77 provides that the author has the right of paternity, ie the right to be identified as the author of the literary, dramatic, musical or artistic work or as the director of the film. The second moral right is the right of integrity which entitles the author or director to prevent his work from being treated in a derogatory fashion in terms of s 80(1) of CDPA. The provisions of s 80(2)(b) of CDPA state that the author's or director's work is treated in a derogatory manner if it is distorted or mutilated or is otherwise treated in a manner which is prejudicial to the honour or reputation of the author or director. Section 84 of CDPA also provides the author with the right not to have a literary, dramatic, musical or artistic work falsely attributed to him as author or director. Section 85 of CDPA also provides that a person who for private and domestic purposes commissions the taking of a photograph or the making of a film has a right of privacy in respect of such works, where copyright subsists in the resulting works. However, the right of privacy does not confer a separate right of ownership in copyright in favour of that person who commissioned the work. Finally in terms of reg 3 of the Artist's Resale Right Regulations 2006 (SI 2006/346), the creators of works of graphic or plastic art such as a picture, a collage, a painting, a drawing, an engraving, a print, a lithograph, a sculpture, a tapestry, a ceramic, an item of glassware or a photograph, enjoy a right ("resale right") to a royalty on any sale of the work which is a resale subsequent to the first transfer of ownership by the author.

It is not possible to alienate a moral right except where the person entitled to the moral right is deceased. Moral rights, with the exception of the resale right under reg 3 of the Artist's Resale Right Regulations 2006 (SI 2006/346) may be waived. All moral rights endure for the same period as the economic rights, except for the false attribution right under s 84 of CDPA, which endures for 20 years after the death of the author or director. The holder of a moral right has the right to be protected against any infringement which is to be treated as a breach of a statutory duty in terms of s 103(1) of CDPA. However, whether this means that remedies other than the usual remedies are available on a civil action is unclear.

Protection from primary and secondary infringement

The copyright owner has the benefit of two forms of protection, namely the right to be protected in respect of primary infringement and secondary infringement. With regard to primary infringement, in terms of s 16 of CDPA, the copyright owner has the exclusive right to do certain acts in relation to the works in the UK, namely:

- to copy the work;
- to issue copies of the work to the public;
- to perform, show or play the work in public;
- to broadcast the work or include it in a cable programme service; or
- to make an adaptation of the work or do any of the other restricted acts in relation to an adaptation.

In the event that the above acts are performed by a third party without the consent of the copyright owner, the right has been infringed. In terms of s 24 of CDPA, secondary infringement describes the situation when a third party deals in infringing copies of copyright works without the licence of the copyright owner. Secondary infringement involves the situation where the third party provides the means for making infringing copies, permitting the use of premises for infringing performances and the provision of apparatus for infringing performances.

The coverage of the protection enjoyed by the copyright owner is limited to the right to prevent the copying of the work. Thus, it stands to reason that copyright does not enable the copyright owner to take action against a person who independently creates the same work, eg inadvertently. Moreover, it should be stressed that copyright arises automatically by operation of law. There is no requirement for registration in order to constitute copyright. Finally, it is also possible for copyright to be owned jointly by more than one person.

PATENTS

Introduction

The regulation of patents is governed by CDPA, the Patents Act 1977 ("the 1977 Act") and the Patents Act 2004 ("the 2004 Act"). A patent right may be granted in respect of an invention. Section 1(1) of the 1977 Act stipulates that a patent may be granted only for an invention in respect of which certain conditions are satisfied, namely that the invention is new, involves an inventive step and is capable of industrial application. Further, by virtue of s 1(3) of the 1977 Act, it is provided that a patent must not be granted for an invention the commercial exploitation of which would be contrary to public policy or morality.

"New", "inventive step"

Section 2(1) states that an invention will be taken to be new if it does not form part of the state of the art at the priority date (which is stipulated as commonly being the date of filing of the application for registration of the patent in terms of s 5 of the 1977 Act), the state of the art comprising all matter by written or oral description by use or in any other way. With regard to what is meant by an "inventive step", the relevant provision is s 3 of the 1977 Act which directs that an inventive step will be one which is not obvious to a person skilled in the art, having regard to any matter which forms part of the state of the art, ie it must introduce a new idea to the state of knowledge existing at the time. Section 4 directs that the requirement that the inventive step be capable of industrial application means that it must be capable of being made or used in any kind of industry, including agriculture, that is to say that it performs a useful technical purpose.

Exceptions

In terms of ss 1(2) and 4A(1) of the 1977 Act, certain things are deemed not to be patentable inventions: first, anything which consists of a discovery, scientific theory or mathematical method; secondly, a method of treatment of the human or animal body by surgery or therapy, or a method of diagnosis practised on the human or animal body; thirdly, a literary, dramatic, musical or artistic work or any other aesthetic creation; fourthly, a scheme, rule or method for performing a mental act; fifthly, playing a game or doing business; and, finally, a program for a computer and the presentation of information.

Registration

It will commonly be the person who has created the invention who will become the registered owner of a patent. However, this is not always the case. For example, in terms of s 39 of the 1977 Act, an employer will be deemed to own an invention and have the right to register it as a patent where it is created by his employee, *inter alia*, in the course of the employee's normal duties and an invention might reasonably be expected to result from the carrying out of those duties. In order to be patented, an invention must be registered with the UK Intellectual Property Office ("UKIPO") in respect of a UK patent or the European Patent Office for a patent in respect of certain identified European countries. An application for a patent is made in accordance with s 14 of the 1977 Act. Section 14 provides that every application for a patent must be set out in the prescribed form and filed at the UKIPO duly containing a request for the grant of a patent, a specification containing a description of the invention, a claim or claims defining the extent of the monopoly sought by the inventor and any drawing referred to in the description or any claim together with an abstract. Section 14(3) of the 1977 Act stipulates that the specification must disclose the invention in a manner which is clear enough and complete enough for the invention to be reproduced by a person skilled in the art. The claim or claims within the specification must define the matter for which the applicant seeks protection, be clear and concise, be supported by the description and relate to one invention or to a group of inventions which are so linked as to form a single inventive concept.

Pre-registration screening

When the UKIPO receives the application, it is subjected to a process of preliminary examination by an examiner in order to determine whether the requirements of the 1977 Act have been satisfied all in accordance with s 15A of the 1977 Act. The terms of s 16 of the 1977 Act provide for subsequent publication of the application as it was filed. A substantive examination and search of the application is then made in accordance with ss 17 and 18 of the 1977 Act and the examiner will then decide whether to grant and publish the application in its final form. In terms of s 24 of the 1977 Act, as soon as practicable after a patent has been granted, a notice that the patent has been granted must be published and a certificate in the prescribed form must be sent to the proprietor of the patent that the patent has been granted to the proprietor. Once granted, by virtue of s 25 of the 1977 Act, a patent will take effect from the date of filing of the application for a period of up to 20 years.

Nature of right

Section 31(2) of the 1977 Act directs that a patent right is a form of incorporeal moveable property in terms of Scots law. The owner of the patent has the right to sell it or license it to third parties in return for the payment of royalties, etc. The patent right confers a right in favour of the patent owner to prevent third parties from using the invention for a period of up to 20 years in the UK, ie an exclusionary right. The patent does not always confer a positive right to exploit the invention, eg where the patent improves upon an invention which was already patented.

Protection from infringement

Section 60(1) of the 1977 Act governs the circumstances in which a third party will be deemed to have infringed a patent owner's patent. First, a third party infringes a patent over a product where he makes, disposes of, offers to dispose of, uses or imports that product or keeps it whether for disposal or otherwise in the UK without the consent of the owner of the patent. Secondly, a third party infringes a patent in respect of a process where he uses the process or offers it for use in the United Kingdom when he knows, or it is obvious to a reasonable person in the circumstances, that its use there without the consent of the proprietor would be an infringement of the patent. Thirdly, a third party will be deemed to have infringed a patent for a process where he disposes of, offers to dispose of, uses or imports any product obtained directly by means of that process or keeps any such product whether for disposal or otherwise in the UK without the consent of the owner of the patent. Finally, a third party also infringes a patent for an invention if, while the patent is in force and without the consent of the proprietor, he supplies or offers to supply in the UK a person (other than a licensee or other person entitled to work the invention) with any of the means, relating to an essential element of the invention, for putting the invention into effect when he knows, or it is obvious to a reasonable person in the circumstances, that those means are suitable for putting, and are intended to put, the invention into effect in the UK.

Exceptions

However, there are exceptions to infringement set out in s 60(5) of the 1977 Act which provides that a third party will not be guilty of infringement in circumstances where the use of the patent is done by the third party privately and for non-commercial purposes or for experimental purposes relating to the subject matter of the invention, amongst other matters. In order to prove infringement, the specification and claim of the patent owner is compared against the product or process of the defender. Whether the product or process of the third party amounts to an infringement is essentially a factual test, but it need not be identical in order to amount to an infringement. The case of *Gormully and Jeffery Manufacturing Co v North British Rubber Co Ltd* (1898) demonstrates that the courts will apply the "pith and marrow" doctrine to the effect that the court will separate the essential features of the specification from the inessential features. Where the essential aspects of the specification are copied, then infringement is established even though the final product differs as regards the features of the specification which are inessential.

TRADE MARKS

Introduction

Section 1(1) of the Trade Marks Act 1994 ("the 1994 Act") directs that a trade mark is any sign capable of being represented graphically which is capable of distinguishing goods or services of one undertaking from those of other undertakings. Once registered, the trade mark represents a property right which is vested in the proprietor and the proprietor is entitled to various protections, namely the right and remedies contained in the 1994 Act. In terms of s 22 of the 1994 Act, a registered trade mark is a form of incorporeal moveable property. In order to be registered, the trade mark must not fall within the grounds for the refusal of a registration. Thus, by virtue of s 3 of the 1994 Act, the trade mark must have a distinctive character, it must not be descriptive of the underlying goods or services which it represents and it must not represent a customary articulation of the trade. Moreover, it is provided in s 3(2) and (3) of the 1994 Act that a sign must not be registered as a trade mark if it consists exclusively of the shape which results from the nature of the goods themselves, the shape of goods which is necessary to obtain a technical result or the shape which gives substantial value to the goods. Moreover, registration of a trade mark will be refused if it is contrary to public policy or to accepted principles of morality or it is of such a nature as to deceive the public as to the nature, quality or geographical origin of the goods or service.

Grounds of refusal

Section 5 of the 1994 Act also provides for certain relative grounds for the refusal of registration of the trade mark. First, a trade mark must not be registered if it is identical with an earlier trade mark and the goods or services for which the trade mark is applied for are identical with the goods or services for which the earlier trade mark is protected. Secondly, registration will be refused where the mark is identical with an earlier trade mark and is to be registered for goods or services similar to those for which the earlier trade mark is protected or where the mark is similar to an earlier trade mark and is to be registered for goods or services identical with or similar to those for which the earlier trade mark is protected and, in both circumstances, there exists a likelihood of confusion on the part of the public, which includes the likelihood of association with the earlier trade mark. Thirdly, a trade mark will be refused registration where it is identical with or similar to an earlier trade mark if or to the extent that the earlier trade mark has a reputation in the UK and the use of the later mark without due cause would take unfair advantage of, or be detrimental to, the distinctive character or repute of the earlier trade mark. Finally, a trade mark must be refused registration if its use in the UK is liable to be prevented by virtue of any rule of law (eg the law of passing off) which protects an unregistered trade mark or other sign used in the course of trade or by virtue of an earlier right other than those referred to above, in particular by virtue of the law of copyright, design right or registered designs.

Registration

In the UK, an application for registration of a trade mark is made with the UKIPO. The UKIPO will examine for earlier UK trade marks, EC trade marks or international trade marks protected in the UK or the EC which conflict with the application. If such conflicting marks are identified, the applicant and the prior registrants will be notified. The applicant then has the right to choose whether to continue with his application, to alter it or to seek the approval of the prior registrant to the application. Sections 42 and 43 of the Trade Marks Act 1994 stipulate that a registered trade mark receives protection from conflicting registrations and infringement for a period of 10 years, which may be renewed for further periods of 10 years. For example, the first ever trade mark registered in 1876 has been renewed many times and is still on the Register today.

Protection from infringement

Section 10 of the 1994 Act deals with the infringement of registered trade marks. It is stated that a person infringes a registered trade mark if he uses in the course of trade a sign which is identical with the trade mark in relation to goods or services which are identical with those for which it is registered. Section 10(2) of the 1994 Act builds on s 10(1) to the effect that a person infringes a registered trade mark if he uses in the course of trade a sign where, because the sign is identical with the trade mark and is used in relation to goods or services similar to those for which the trade mark is registered or the sign is similar to the trade mark and is used in relation to goods or services identical with or similar to those for which the trade mark is registered, there exists a likelihood of confusion on the part of the public, which includes the likelihood of association with the trade mark. A person also infringes a registered trade mark if he uses a sign in the course of trade which is identical to or similar to the trade mark, where the trade mark has a reputation in the UK and the use of the sign (without due cause) takes unfair advantage of, or is detrimental to, the distinctive character or the repute of the trade mark. However, in terms of s 11 of the 1994 Act, where a person uses a registered trade mark in accordance with honest practices in industrial or commercial matters, the trade mark is not infringed where that person uses his own name or address, or the use concerns the kind, quality, quantity, intended purpose, value, geographical origin, the time of production of goods or of rendering of services, or other characteristics of goods or services, or the use is necessary to indicate the intended purposes of a product or service, eg as accessories or spare parts. This section entitles a rival trade to engage in comparative advertising, provided that the use complies with the requirements of "honest practices".

Remedies for infringement

Section 14 of the 1994 Act regulates the raising of actions for infringement. If successful, the remedies of damages, interdict, count, reckoning and payment, and all other usual remedies in relation to the infringement of property rights are available to the successful trade mark owner. The court also has the power under s 15 of the 1994 Act to order the erasure, removal or obliteration of the offending sign or the destruction of the infringing goods, articles or material where such erasure, removal or obliteration is not reasonably practicable. Finally, by virtue of the provisions of s 16 of the 1994 Act, a trade mark owner may apply to the court for an order for the delivery to him of any infringing material or articles which a person has in his possession, custody or control in the course of a business.

DESIGN RIGHTS

Design rights may be protected under CDPA or the Registered Designs Act 1949 ("the 1949 Act"). In the latter case, the design is registered, whereas in the former it is not. Design rights arise by operation of law without registration under CDPA. Section 213(2) of CDPA directs that "design" means the design of any aspect of the shape or configuration (whether internal or external) of the whole or part of an article. Thus, there is no requirement to demonstrate that the design is appealing to the eye in any way. Registered designs under the 1949 Act are much stronger than CDPA in the protection which they afford designers. Section 1 of the 1949 Act directs that the extent of the protection of the "design" is wide enough to encompass the appearance of the whole or a part of a product resulting from the features of, in particular, the lines, contours, colours, shape, texture or materials of the product or its ornamentation. Section 1B of the 1949 Act goes on to stipulate that the design must be new (in the sense that no identical design or no design whose features differ only in immaterial details has been made available to the public before the relevant date) and possess individual character (by which is meant that the overall impression it produces on the informed user differs from the overall impression produced on such a user by any design which has been made available to the public before the relevant date, taking into account the degree of freedom of the author in creating the design). This can be understood in terms of a requirement that the design must be appealing to the eye in order to be eligible for registration under the 1949 Act. Thus, in terms of s 1C of the 1949 Act, a design which is solely dictated by the nature of its technical function will not be registrable under the 1949 Act.

Essential Facts

- The main types of intellectual property right which are recognised by the law are copyright, patents, trade marks and designs.
- Copyright may exist in literary, dramatic, musical or artistic works, films, broadcasts, sound recordings and typographical arrangements of published works.
- There is a requirement that the literary, dramatic, musical or artistic work be "original" and "recorded, in writing or otherwise" in terms of ss 1(1)(a) and 3(2) of CDPA.
- The right of copyright is comprised of two components, namely the economic right and the moral right.
- A patent may be granted only for an invention in respect of which certain conditions are satisfied, namely that the invention is new, involves an inventive step, and is capable of industrial application; and its commercial exploitation must not be contrary to public policy or morality.
- A trade mark is any sign capable of being represented graphically which is capable of distinguishing goods or services of one undertaking from those of other undertakings.
- Design rights may be protected under CDPA or the Registered Designs Act 1949.

Essential Cases

University of London Press Ltd v University Tutorial Press Ltd (1916): held that exam papers would attract copyright protection as "original literary works".

10 DILIGENCE

Where an unsecured creditor provides a service or supplies goods to a debtor and raises an invoice, in an ideal world, the creditor would be able to be ensure payment is forthcoming without taking any action. In most cases, this is what will happen. But not always. Where a debtor fails to pay or refuses to pay, there are two legal options available to an unsecured creditor. The first is to petition for the sequestration or liquidation of the debtor, ie to seek to bankrupt the debtor. Needless to say, this is fairly extreme. The second option is to do diligence over the assets of the debtor in order to secure payment of the invoice. There are a number of diligences available to an unsecured creditor and they each involve a judicial process. When completed, diligence thus amounts to a judicial form of security, ie a right in security in favour of the unsecured creditor over the assets of the debtor under judicial supervision.

THE TYPES OF DILIGENCE AVAILABLE

There are four principal forms of diligence. These four diligences can be best understood by dividing them into two camps: first, according to the type of property over which they are available; and, secondly, in accordance with the nature of the action taken over the property, ie whether it entitles the creditor to *freeze* the debtor's use of the property or whether it enables them to *seize* that asset from the debtor.

Contrast with bankruptcy

Diligence can be contrasted with the bankruptcy process. Unlike diligence, bankruptcy is a procedure which seeks to protect all of the debtor's creditors. In the case of bankruptcy, all (subject to limited exceptions) of the assets of the debtor are vested in the trustee and the distribution of funds by the trustee is undertaken on the basis of equality. ie the *pari passu* principle applies. Another difference is that bankruptcy entails the involvement of a third party in the process known as a trustee, whereas diligence involves no intermediary. Thus, in contrast with bankruptcy, diligence is a particularly "selfish" process which enables one unsecured creditor to secure an advantage over the other unsecured creditors of the debtor and for that reason it is akin to a right in security, albeit under the auspices of judicial supervision.

Attachment

The first diligence to mention is attachment which is used principally against corporeal moveable assets. Attachment replaced the diligence formerly known as poinding. Attachment ultimately leads to the sale of the debtor's property. The proceeds of sale are then applied by the creditor towards the repayment of the debts owed by the debtor to the creditor. As will become apparent, certain corporeal moveables are exempted from the diligence of attachment. The relevant legislation governing attachment is contained in Part 2 of the Debt Arrangement and Attachment (Scotland) Act 2002 ("the 2002 Act") (to be amended by Part 13 of the Bankruptcy and Diligence (Scotland) Act 2007 ("the 2007 Act")).

Arrestment

Arrestment is available over corporeal and incorporeal moveable assets, eg ships and cargo owned by the debtor, the goods of the debtor held in the hands of a third party, the funds of the debtor held by a bank in a bank account and the earnings of a debtor held by the debtor's employer.

Inhibition

The third diligence to mention is inhibition. Inhibition is available over the corporeal heritable property of a debtor. It is a "freeze" diligence in the sense that it does not result in the transfer of the debtor's property to the creditor. Instead, it disentitles the debtor from dealing with the inhibited asset. An inhibition can only be exercised by a creditor over the heritable assets of a debtor.

Adjudication

Finally, the diligence of adjudication for debt ("adjudication") must be mentioned. Adjudication can also be exercised over the heritage of the debtor. However, unlike inhibition, it is a "seize" diligence to the effect that it entitles the creditor to seize the heritage of the debtor and vests the real right to the heritable property in the creditor. Adjudication will be abolished when s 79 of the 2007 Act comes into force and, by virtue of s 81 of the 2007 Act, it will be replaced by a diligence to be known as "land attachment".

Other diligences

Other diligences to be introduced are "money attachment" and "residual attachment" when ss 174–198 and 129–145 of the 2007 Act are fully introduced. It is intended that these two new diligences will cover assets of the debtor which do not fall within the scope of the other diligences, ie to cover the existing "cracks" in the pre-2007 Act Scots law of diligence. Other diligences known to Scots common law such as real poinding, real adjudication and sequestration for rent (see s 208 of the 2007 Act) have been abolished and diligences such as maills and duties will be abolished in terms of s 207 of the 2007 Act when ss 81–128 of the 2007 Act, introducing the diligence of land attachment, come into force. For that reason, those diligences will not be considered in this book.

ENFORCEMENT OF DILIGENCE

In order to execute diligence, a creditor appoints a sheriff officer or messenger at arms. Section 60 of the 2007 Act provides that sheriff officers and messengers at arms will be abolished and replaced with judicial officers in terms of s 57 of the 2007 Act. The regime envisaged that the Lord President would appoint judicial officers under a recommendation by a newly introduced regulatory body known as the Scottish Civil Enforcement Commission. However, these provisions have not been introduced and, at the time of writing, it is unlikely that they will ever come into force.

PRIORITY AND EFFECT OF DILIGENCE

As explained above, diligences executed over the assets of the debtor rank in accordance with the date of execution of diligence in accordance with the *prior tempore potior iure* principle (see Erskine, *Institute*, III, 6, 1). Thus, it is important to stress that the priority of diligences is dictated neither by the date on which the debt owed by the debtor to the creditor was constituted, nor by the date of the court decree. The effect of a creditor executing diligence over an individual asset of the debtor is such that the creditor is given a real right in security over that asset. However, this is subject to one exception, namely inhibition.

It is not possible to execute diligence against a debtor where the individual asset is owned by a third party, eg where a third party's assets are possessed by the debtor in the debtor's home. Where a third party enjoys some right in the property of the debtor, the interaction between those third party rights and the diligence requires to be examined. The nature of the third party right and the diligence affects the outcome. First, where the asset is co-owned by the debtor and a third party, the diligence is subject to the rights of the co-owner. Secondly, where a third party is the holder of a *ius in re aliena* over the individual asset such as a real right in security, lease or servitude, that *ius in re aliena* is unaffected by the diligence provided it was constituted prior to that diligence. Thirdly, with the exception of inhibition, the personal rights of third parties over the assets of the debtor are defeated, eg where a debtor enters into a contract to sell an asset to a third party and diligence is executed over that asset, the rights of the third party to have that asset conveyed to him are defeated, even in circumstances where the third party has paid the purchase price. Finally, it is not possible to execute diligence over assets owned by the debtor which are held in trust for a beneficiary. This applies whether the trust is patent or latent (*Heritable Reversionary Co Ltd* v *Millar* (1892)).

ATTACHMENT

Introduction

The first diligence to consider is attachment, which was formerly referred to as poinding. It is recognised as a form of diligence which is available over corporeal moveable property for recovery of money owed in terms of s 10(1) of the 2002 Act. In order to be effective, attachment must follow an execution of a decree or a document of debt and only upon property owned (whether alone or in common) by the debtor. Attachment is only competent where the debtor has been served with a charge for payment (except where a summary warrant is served), the period for payment specified in the charge has expired without payment being made and, where the debtor is an individual, the creditor has, no earlier than 12 weeks before taking any steps to execute the attachment, provided the debtor with a debt advice and information package.

Restricted articles

Section 11 of the 2002 Act stipulates certain articles which cannot be attached, eg the debtor's tools of trade, books, vehicles used in the course of the debtor's business, garden tools, etc, and attachment cannot be conducted on Sundays or public holidays or before 8 am or after 8 pm. If the debtor's assets are contained within his dwellinghouse, Part 3 of the 2002 Act provides that a creditor must first obtain an exceptional attachment order before attaching non-essential assets such as clothing, medical aids, medical equipment, children's toys, articles reasonably required for the care or upbringing of a child, beds, bedding, household linen, chairs, settees, tables, lights, light fittings and other materials itemised in Sch 2 to the 2002 Act.

Procedure

In the event that the assets are located outwith the dwellinghouse of the debtor, or within mobile homes which are not the only or principal residence of the debtor, a special procedure exists in terms of ss 14–19 of the 2002 Act. The procedures enable sheriff officers to open lockfast places. Moreover, in terms of s 19A of the 2002 Act, a procedure exists which entitles sheriff officers to remove certain assets from the debtor's property without notice where there is an element of urgency involved and it is necessary to do so to preserve the value of the asset. An attachment must be reported to the court and the debtor is entitled to make payment to have the attached articles redeemed. Where the debtor fails to pay, the creditor has the power to remove the assets and have them publicly auctioned.

Interim attachment

Section 9A of the 2002 Act introduces a power which enables the court to grant warrant for diligence by attachment of corporeal moveable property owned (whether alone or in common) by the debtor on the dependence of an action, ie where the creditor raises an action or proceedings against the debtor, it is possible for the creditor to exercise attachment over an asset or assets of the debtor in security of the action. Such attachment is known as interim attachment. Section 9A(2) of the 2002 Act directs that a warrant for interim attachment is competent only where an action contains a conclusion for payment of a sum other than by way of expenses.

Restricted articles

Like attachment, there are various restrictions on the nature of the articles which can be subjected to interim attachment and these are specified in s 9B of the 2002 Act: eg a mobile home which is the only or principal residence of a person other than the debtor, any article of a perishable nature or which is likely to deteriorate substantially and rapidly in condition or value and any article acquired by the debtor to be sold by the debtor or as a material for a process of manufacturing for sale by the debtor, in the ordinary course of that trade.

ARRESTMENT

Arrestment in execution

The next diligence to consider is arrestment. Arrestment may be in execution or on the dependence of an action. There are two forms of arrestment, namely "ordinary arrestment" and "arrestment of goods". Ordinary arrestment is a diligence which is available over the incorporeal moveable assets of the debtor. The most common assets of the debtor to be arrested are his bank accounts and shares. The creditor is referred to as the "arrester", the debtor is known as "the common debtor" and the final party is the "arrestee", ie the party who owes obligations to the common debtor, against whom the common debtor has certain rights and in whose hands the arrestment is made. Thus, the diligence of arrestment involves three parties – the creditor/arrester, the common debtor and the debtor of the common debtor – and in that sense it is tripartite in nature. In the case of competing arrestments, the *prior tempore potior iure* principle applies.

Procedure

The procedure for initiating the diligence of arrestment is set out in s 73A of the Debtors (Scotland) Act 1987 ("the 1987 Act"). It is provided that an arrestment in execution must follow a decree in respect of the debt due to the creditor and a schedule of arrestment must be served upon the common debtor together with debt advice and information. The service of a schedule of arrestment on the common debtor serves to attach all of the assets of the arrestee listed on the schedule in favour of the arrester. Section 73E of the 1987 Act provides that the arrestment attaches the lesser of (a) the sum due by the arrestee to the debtor or (b) the sum due by the debtor to the arrester, plus expenses, and interest. Thus, it is not possible for a creditor to arrest more than the principal sum, plus interest and expenses, which it is due from the debtor.

Effect on incorporeal moveables

When the incorporeal moveable assets of the common debtor are arrested, they are effectively frozen and the common debtor is unable to deal with those assets. If the arrestee also holds corporeal moveables as well as funds the arrestment will attach the moveables if the funds are insufficient. Otherwise, corporeal moveables cannot be arrested. The incorporeal moveables are frozen in the sense that when a creditor arrests the bank account of the common debtor, the common debtor is unable to deal with the funds in that account, eg to withdraw those funds. Section 73F places limits on the amount which can be arrested whereby in circumstances where the arrestment is of an individual's bank account a prescribed minimum balance cannot be arrested. Moreover, it should be recalled that the amount arrested cannot exceed the value of the debt due to the creditor/arrester.

Automatic release

Funds arrested are automatically released from the arrestee to the creditor after 14 weeks from the service of the decree upon the common debtor or the date of arrestment in terms of s 73J of the 1987 Act. However, there is an exception which applies where an objection is made. In such a case, ss 73L, 73M and 73N of the 1987 Act direct that a court hearing must take place. The common debtor will also be entitled to object to the arrestment under s 73Q of the 1987 Act on the basis that it is unduly harsh. A court hearing must then take place in accordance with s 73R of the 1987 Act.

Furthcoming

Before the expiry of the 14-week period, an arrestment may be enforced by an action for furthcoming. Furthcoming serves to convey ownership of the assets arrested from the arrestee to the arrester, ie to seize the arrested assets. Section 95A of the 1987 Act directs that an action for furthcoming must be pursued within a period of 3 years of the date of arrestment.

Other property which can be arrested

Other incorporeal moveable assets of the common debtor such as shares and debts/receivables which are due to the common debtor may also be arrested. A prime example is rent due to a common debtor who is a landlord; in such a case, the arrester may arrest in the hands of the tenant. However, it is not possible to arrest money, such as bank notes, coins, ie cash. Instead, the diligence of money attachment will be available for the purposes of money or cash when it comes into force.

Arrester's rights

When the arrester arrests the incorporeal moveable assets of the common debtor, the arrester can obtain no better rights to the assets than the common debtor had and so the arrestor takes such assets subject to any encumbrances. Thus, if the common debtor has granted a right in security over those assets to a third party, the arrester's rights in the assets arrested are taken subject to the rights of the secured third party. Conversely, the arrestment cannot operate to make the arrester's position worse than if he had not arrested.

Acquirenda

The general rule is that *acquirenda* cannot be arrested, ie things or rights acquired by the debtor after the time of arrestment (Erskine, *Institute*, III, 6, 18). The effect of this rule is that where a bank account with no funds is arrested on 16 February 2009, this is ineffective to arrest funds which are credited to the common debtor's account on 17 February 2009. However, *acquirenda* and future debts should neither be conflated nor confused. It is possible to arrest future debts, ie debts which presently exist, but which are not due to be paid until some date in the future (*Stair Memorial Encyclopaedia*, vol 8, para 268). The classic example is contractual sums due to be paid under a loan agreement. Moreover, an arrestment catches only the existing asset arrested. For example, if an arrester on day 1 arrests the common debtor's bank account and there is a balance of £1,000, this is attached. However, if £50,000 is credited to the common debtor's bank account on day 2, this not attached.

Effect of arrestment

There are two competing theories regarding the effect of an arrestment: ie Scots law is unclear as to which theory applies, but it is generally thought that the second theory is preferred. The first theory is that an arrestment acts as a signal to the arrestee which prohibits the arrestee from transferring possession of the asset to the common debtor, ie the arrestee is prohibited from enabling the common debtor to deal with his asset(s) which has been arrested. Thus, this first theory is known as the "prohibition theory" (see *Lord Advocate* v *Royal Bank of Scotland* (1977) and *Iona Hotels Ltd* v *Craig* (1990)). The second theory is referred to as the "attachment theory". In terms of the attachment theory, an arrestment is something more than a simple instruction to the arrestee prohibiting them from enabling the common debtor to deal with the arrested assets. Instead, the effect of an arrestment is to set down a nexus on the subject arrested. In the case of funds arrested, an arrestment is tantamount to a conditional assignation of the funds to the arrester, which condition will be purified when the process of furthcoming is effectively completed in the future. On the other hand, an arrestment of goods is treated as if the arrester has been conferred with a real right in security over those arrested goods (see *Lindsay* (1860) and *Inglis* (1898)). In most cases, nothing will come of the difference in analysis between the prohibition and attachment theories. However, in complex cases, the outcome will diverge depending on which theory is applicable.

Multiplepoinding

Multiplepoinding is an institution separate from arrestment and arises where the holder of a fund of money or property, known as a fund *in medio*, is the subject of a number of competing claims from creditors. The process enables the arrestee, ie the holder of the fund, to place matters in the hands of the court. A pre-condition to doing so is that there have been multiple arrestments of the same funds or property in the hands of the arrestee. The court then deals with the claims and directs how such funds should be applied.

Arrestment of goods

Arrestment of goods is particularly important in circumstances where the goods of the common debtor are held by a third party, eg in a warehouse or storage facility. Of course, in such circumstances, the diligence of attachment is also available. However, the main difference is that there is no requirement to inventorise the goods in the case of an arrestment of goods.

INHIBITIONS

Inhibition is a diligence which is available over the heritage of the common debtor. When effected, the diligence covers the entirety of the common debtor's heritage. An inhibition is not effective to confer a real right in favour of the creditor. Instead, the rights which are given to a creditor are determined by common law rules and the 2007 Act. In essence, an inhibition is a "freeze" diligence, ie the heritage inhibited is deemed litigious, but does not transfer title in the heritage to the creditor.

Effect of inhibition

Section 149 of the 2007 Act introduced s 155 of the Titles to Land Consolidation (Scotland) Act 1868 to the effect that an inhibition only takes effect once it has been registered in the Register of Inhibitions. However, this is subject to an exception which is applicable in circumstances where a notice of inhibition is registered in advance and the inhibition is registered within 21 days thereof. In terms of s 148 of the 2007 Act, an inhibition is registered only by registering a schedule of inhibition and the certificate of execution of the inhibition in the Register of Inhibitions under the common debtor's name. Section 154 of the 2007 Act stipulates that an inhibition does not give any preference in insolvency.

Procedure

Inhibitions can be used to enforce decrees or documents of debt and letters of inhibition will no longer be competent in the Court of Session.

An inhibitor will be under an obligation to serve a debt and information package upon the common debtor before an inhibition becomes effective.

The implications of an inhibition

There are three principal implications of the grant of an inhibition.

No right to alienate

First, in terms of s 160 of the 2007 Act, the common debtor is precluded from selling or alienating the heritable property which he owns or granting a deed which affects the property. This is subject to the exception in s 159 of the 2007 Act that purchasers in good faith will not be affected by the inhibition. Subject to s 159, any contravention on the part of the common debtor is that the alienation is voidable at the behest of the inhibitor, ie it is not automatically void *ab initio*. The inhibitor has the ability to reduce, ie annul, the conveyance *ex capite inhibitionis* only in a question with the inhibitor. However, if a disposition or heritable security is granted by the common debtor contrary to the inhibition, this disposition or security is still good against other parties, on the basis that reduction applies "*ad hunc effectum*" and is not "catholic".

No power to grant security

Secondly, the common debtor is disentitled from granting any security over the heritage. Where this rule is contravened, the repercussions are identical to those applicable in the case of an alienation noted above.

Postponement of new creditor

Thirdly, if a common debtor borrows sums subsequent to the date of inhibition, the new creditor is effectively postponed to the inhibitor vis-à-vis the common debtor's heritage.

Ranking of inhibitions

With regard to the ranking of inhibitions, the rules are authoritatively detailed in Bell's *Commentaries*, II, 413, under the heading "Canons of Ranking of Bell" (see also *Scottish Waggon Co* (1906)). There are three stages which must be negotiated in order to ascertain the ranking of inhibitions. In the first case, the parties rank on the assumption that the inhibition did not exist. For example, if A and B are owed £100,000 and £300,000 respectively from Z, A inhibits Z's property and Z subsequently borrows £200,000 from C, if Z is sequestrated and the assets are heritable and amount to £60,000, if there was no inhibition, A would receive £10,000, B £30,000 and C £20,000. At the second stage, one must determine what the inhibitor would receive if the post-inhibition loan of C did not exist. In such a situation, A would receive £15,000 and B would get £45,000. At the final stage, one must then calculate how the assets would be distributed on the basis that (i) B is unaffected by the inhibition as a pre-inhibition creditor and (ii) A as inhibitor is entitled to draw back from C the sum which is required to give him the sum of £15,000. On this basis, B would receive £30,000, A £15,000 and C £15,000.

Future voluntary acts

It is important to stress that an inhibition only strikes down the future voluntary acts of the common debtor. Where a notice of inhibition is registered in the Register of Inhibitions on the same day that the common debtor has concluded missives to sell heritage, the effect of *Park, Petitioners* (2008) is that the inhibition is deemed to take effect from the conclusion of the day on which it, or the prior notice, was registered. On that basis, the missives are not struck at by the inhibition and the parties may proceed to sell and purchase. In the case of a sale of heritage by a heritable creditor, an inhibition does not prevent such a sale. In order to profit from the inhibition, the inhibitor must either (1) have adjudged before the date of sale or (2) have arrested the free proceeds after that date. Inhibitions prescribe in terms of s 24 of the Conveyancing (Scotland) Act 1924 after 5 years and they have no effect on any heritage acquired after the date of their registration in terms of s 157 of the Titles to Land Consolidation (Scotland) Act 1868.

ADJUDICATION AND LAW REFORM

An action for adjudication may follow an inhibition. It is an action which must be raised in the Court of Session and the court's decree must be registered in the Land Register. Unlike an inhibition, adjudication is a seize diligence. However, it is not effective to transfer title to the heritage to the adjudger and so the creditor retains ownership of the heritage. Rather, the effect of an adjudication is to confer a judicial right in security in favour of the adjudger. The effect is that the creditor is unable to convey the heritage but has the power to evict the common debtor from the property and have it let out to a third party. Where the property has already been let by the common debtor to a third party, the adjudger is entitled to the rents on the basis of maills and duties.

Acquisition of ownership

Where the debt remains unpaid for a period of 10 years, the adjudger has the power to acquire ownership of the heritage by obtaining a declarator from the court. However, in reality, this is unlikely to happen, since the debtor may pay beforehand, the rents obtained may pay off the debt, a prior heritable creditor may sell the property or the common debtor may be sequestrated or liquidated. Adjudications rank according to the date of their registration.

Law reform

When ss 79–128 of the 2007 Act come into force, they will modify the legal position. Section 79 of the 2007 Act stipulates that the diligence of adjudication will be abolished. It will be replaced by two new diligences, namely land attachment and residual attachment. Since these provisions are not yet in force, they will not be considered here.

DILIGENCE ON THE DEPENDENCE AND INTERIM DILIGENCES

In discussing the diligences below, it has been assumed that they were being pursued by a creditor in execution – that is to say, that a proven liquid debt is owed by the common debtor to the creditor doing diligence in execution, eg where the debt is admitted by the common debtor and the creditor has already secured a decree from the court which recognises the existence of that debt. However, it is also possible for a creditor to do diligence on the dependence of an action. In such a case, the creditor pursuing an action does not have a decree from the court. Instead the diligence is sought as part of a pursuer's court action and attaches as soon as the action is initiated. Unless it is recalled, the diligence remains in place throughout the process of the court action. Essentially, the property attached by the diligence on the dependence acts as security for the sums claimed by the pursuer under the principal court action – if the pursuer is successful in his court action, those funds or property attached will then be available to satisfy the claim.

Arrestment and inhibition on the dependence

Section 15D of the 1987 Act stipulates that the diligences of arrestment and inhibition may be sought by a pursuer on the dependence of an action or a petition. However, there is one exception, to the extent that an arrestment on the dependence is not competent in the case of earnings. If the pursuer is successful in his court action and is awarded a decree from the court, the diligence transforms from a diligence on the dependence into a diligence in execution. However, if the action is unsuccessful, the diligence on the dependence is determined. Whilst the action is in process, it is not possible for furthcoming to be undertaken in respect of an arrestment on the dependence.

Criteria for grant

The court will grant an arrestment or inhibition on the dependence of an action in the event that the criteria specified in ss 15E(2) (on the basis of no court hearing) or 15F(3) (on the basis of a court hearing) of the 1987 Act are satisfied. That is to say, diligence on the dependence will be granted by the court if (1) it is reasonable in all the circumstances, having regard to the effect granting the arrestment or inhibition on the dependence may have on any person having an interest in the assets and (2) (i) the creditor has a prima facie case on the merits of the action or (ii) there is a real and substantial risk that enforcement of any decree by the creditor would be defeated or prejudiced by the common debtor's insolvency, near insolvency or the debtor removing, disposing, burdening, concealing or otherwise dealing with his assets. The burden of proof falls on the pursuer to satisfy the court that the above criteria have been satisfied.

Interim attachment

Section 173 of the 2007 Act (introducing ss 9A–9S into the 2002 Act) provides for a new diligence on the dependence known as interim attachment. Interim attachment is available in respect of the corporeal moveable assets of the common debtor, subject to certain excepted assets which mirror those exempt from the diligence of attachment in execution. The criteria which the court must apply as a means of forming a decision whether to grant a warrant for interim attachment reflect the same criteria which are applicable in the context of an arrestment or inhibition on the dependence of an action (see above).

Essential Facts

- Diligences may be classified into those which enable a creditor to freeze the debtor's use of the property or seize that asset from the debtor.
- For the purposes of the ranking of diligences, the *prior tempore potior iure* principle applies.
- The principal diligences known to the law of Scotland are attachment, arrestment, furthcoming, inhibition and adjudication (to be replaced by land attachment).
- Attachment is used to do diligence (principally) over the corporeal moveable assets of the debtor.
- Arrestment is available over corporeal and incorporeal moveable assets, eg ships and cargo owned by the debtor, the goods of the debtor held in the hands of a third party, the funds of the debtor held by a bank in a bank account and the earnings of a debtor held by the debtor's employer. It is a "freeze" diligence.
- Furthcoming is a "seize" diligence.
- Inhibition is available over the corporeal heritable property of a debtor. It is a "freeze" diligence.
- An action for adjudication may follow an inhibition.
- Unlike an inhibition, adjudication is a "seize" diligence. However, it is not effective to transfer title to the heritage to the adjudger and so the creditor retains ownership of the heritage. Rather, the effect of an adjudication is to confer a judicial right in security in favour of the adjudger.
- The diligence of adjudication will be replaced by land attachment when Chapter 2 of Part 4 of the 2007 Act comes into force.
- Section 15D of the 1987 Act stipulates that the diligences of arrestment and inhibition may be sought by a pursuer on the dependence of an action or a petition.

Essential Cases

Heritable Reversionary Co Ltd v Millar (1892): it is not possible to execute diligence over assets owned by the debtor which are held in patent or latent trust for a beneficiary.

Lord Advocate v Royal Bank of Scotland (1977) and **Iona Hotels Ltd v Craig (1990)**: authorities for the "prohibition theory" of attachment.

Lindsay (1860) and **Inglis (1898)**: an arrestment of goods is treated as if the arrester has been conferred with a real right in security over those arrested goods.

Park, Petitioners (2008): missives are not struck at by an inhibition registered on the same date.

11 PERSONAL INSOLVENCY

The Scots law of personal insolvency regulates the position of an individual debtor who gets into financial difficulties. While the phrase "personal insolvency" is uncertain in its meaning, it is generally taken to refer to the situation where an individual debtor is unable to meet his liabilities to creditors.

APPLICABLE LEGISLATION

The legislation which applies to personal insolvency is the Bankruptcy (Scotland) Act 1985 ("the 1985 Act") and the Debt Arrangement and Attachment (Scotland) Act 2002. The law of personal insolvency is devolved to the Scottish Parliament in terms of the Scotland Act 1998. It has a bearing on many other areas of private law and commercial law such as property law, the law of diligence, the law of rights in security and trust law. In terms of ss 5 and 6 of the 1985 Act, the personal insolvency regime is applicable to individual living debtors, deceased debtors, trusts, trading or dissolved partnerships and limited partnerships, bodies corporate other than companies incorporated under the Companies Acts and unincorporated bodies such as trade unions and clubs.

THE DEFINITION OF INSOLVENCY

Introduction

In order for an individual to enter into the sequestration process or the law of personal insolvency generally, he must first be "insolvent". There are three types of insolvency.

"Practical insolvency"

The first form of insolvency is practical insolvency. This is not legally defined but is generally treated as covering the situation where a debtor is unable to pay his debts as they fall due. Practical insolvency describes the situation where the debtor is experiencing cash flow problems, eg the debtor has trouble paying his debts.

"Absolute insolvency"

For the purposes of the sequestration and personal insolvency regimes, the relevant concepts are "absolute insolvency" and "apparent insolvency". Section 73(2) of the 1985 Act directs that an individual will be deemed to be "absolutely insolvent" where his total liabilities exceed his total assets. Thus, although an individual is able to pay his debts as they fall due and is experiencing no cash flow difficulties, if he is "balance sheet" insolvent, he will be deemed to be absolutely insolvent. The concept of "absolute insolvency" is particularly relevant for the provisions of the 1985 Act and the common law which confer rights in favour of a trustee in sequestration or the debtor's creditors to challenge certain transactions which the latter entered into prior to the date of his sequestration. These challengeable transactions are referred to as "gratuitous alienations" and "unfair preferences" and will be considered in detail below.

"Apparent insolvency"

The final form of insolvency is "apparent insolvency" which is dealt with by s 7 of the 1985 Act. The concept of "apparent insolvency" is important for the purposes of initiating the process of sequestration and for the termination of contracts. In terms of s 7 of the 1985 Act, apparent insolvency is constituted automatically on the occurrence of the following events:

- where the debtor has been sequestrated or has become bankrupt in any part of the UK or any Member State in the European Union;
- where the debtor provides written notice to creditors that he has ceased to pay his debts as they fall due in the ordinary course of business;
- where the debtor grants a trust deed for behoof of his creditors;
- where a charge for payment has been served on the debtor and the relevant period for payment stipulated therein has expired without payment by the debtor;
- where a decree of adjudication over any part of the debtor's estate has been granted, either for payment or in security;
- where a debt payment programme under the Debt Arrangement and Attachment (Scotland) Act 2002 has been revoked;
- where a creditor of the debtor owed at least the prescribed amount of £750 serves a statutory demand for payment (or demands that the

debtor finds security for payment) on the debtor and there is no (1) denial of the debt by the debtor or (2) payment of the debt (or finding of security for payment) within 3 weeks.

SEQUESTRATION

Introduction

Sequestration describes the process whereby the assets of an insolvent debtor are sold and the proceeds of sale are distributed amongst his creditors. In terms of the sequestration process, the court takes control of all of the estate of the debtor (subject to certain exceptions). The court then passes those assets to a duly qualified and authorised third party for realisation and distribution to creditors in accordance with prescribed rules. That third party is referred to as the trustee in sequestration.

Initiation of court-approved sequestration

The process of sequestration is governed by s 5 of the 1985 Act and is commonly initiated by the presentation of a petition to the sheriff court. Section 5(2)(b) of the 1985 Act stipulates that a petition may be presented by (1) a qualified creditor or creditors, (2) a temporary administrator, (3) a liquidator appointed in another Member State of the European Union, or (4) a trustee acting under a trust deed (provided certain conditions are met). In the case of the presentation of a petition by a qualified creditor or creditors, it is important that the debtor is apparently insolvent within 4 months before the presentation of the petition. A qualified creditor is one who, at the date of the presentation of the petition, is a creditor of the debtor in respect of liquid or illiquid debts, whether secured or unsecured, which amount to not less than £3,000. Where the application for sequestration is by a creditor the creditor is obliged to serve the debtor with a debt information and advice package in terms of s 5(2D) and (2E) of the 1985 Act and s 10(5) of the Debt Arrangement and Attachment (Scotland) Act 2002.

Debtor application procedure

It is now possible for a debtor to be sequestrated without the requirement for the presentation of a petition to the court. The Bankruptcy and Diligence, etc (Scotland) Act 2007 ("the 2007 Act") amended the 1985 Act by introducing the debtor application procedure. This enables debtors to apply to the Accountant in Bankruptcy ("AoB") for their own sequestration in terms of s 5(2A) or (2B) of the 1985 Act. A debtor may make a debtor application with the concurrence of a qualified creditor or qualified creditors. Where the concurrence of a qualified creditor or qualified creditors is not forthcoming, s 5(2B) of the 1985 Act nonetheless enables a debtor to proceed with a debtor application. The debtor may make a debtor application to the AoB where the total amount of his debts is not less than £3,000, an award of sequestration has not been made against him in the period of 5 years ending on the day before the date the debtor application is made, and any one of the following three criteria are satisfied:

- the debtor is apparently insolvent; or
- the debtor is unable to pay his debts and all of the conditions referred to in s 5A of the 1985 Act as amended by the Bankruptcy (Scotland) Act 1985 (Low Income, Low Asset Debtors, etc) Regulations 2008 (SSI 2008/81) are satisfied; or
- the debtor has granted a voluntary trust deed over his estate and the trustee has attempted to make the trust deed protected without success.

Obligations of debtor pursuant to debtor application procedure

A debtor is under an obligation in terms of the Bankruptcy (Scotland) Regulations 2008 (SSI 2008/82) ("the 2008 Regulations") to complete and return a statutory declaration to the AoB which states that the relevant statutory criteria have been satisfied. Any failure to do so will result in the AoB refusing the debtor's application for sequestration unless he is satisfied that the debtor is apparently insolvent. The 2008 Regulations stipulate that the trustee in sequestration appointed must thereafter publicise in the *Edinburgh Gazette* the fact that the debtor has satisfied the criteria for a low income/low assets sequestration in terms of s 5(2A) or (2B) of the 1985 Act.

Criteria for grant of debtor application procedure

Section 12(1) of the 1985 Act directs that the AoB must award sequestration forthwith if the debtor application is made in accordance with the 1985 Act, the debtor has specified in the application that his or its centre of main interests or establishment is located in the UK or another EU Member State, and the debtor has made the application with the concurrence of a qualified creditor or qualified creditors, or, where such concurrence is not forthcoming, the conditions specified in s 5(2B) of the 1985 Act have been complied with. Where the AoB awards sequestration on the making of a debtor application, s 12(4)(a) of the 1985 Act provides that the date of sequestration is the date of the award of sequestration.

Criteria for grant of petition for sequestration by the court

Where a petition for sequestration is presented to the sheriff court, the debtor must be given the chance to defend. This is effected by the sheriff granting a warrant to cite the debtor which calls on the debtor to appear before him to explain why sequestration should not be awarded. Section 12(3A) of the 1985 Act directs that the sheriff must refuse to award sequestration if (1) cause is shown why sequestration cannot competently be awarded or (2) the debtor forthwith pays or satisfies, or produces written evidence of the payment or satisfaction of, or gives or shows that there is sufficient security for the payment of the debt in respect of which he became apparently insolvent and any other debt due by him to the petitioner and any creditor concurring in the petition. Section 12(3) of the 1985 Act directs the sheriff to make the award of sequestration forthwith if he is satisfied that:

- if the debtor has not appeared, proper citation has been made of the debtor;
- the petition has been presented in accordance with the provisions of the 1985 Act;
- a copy of the petition has been sent to the AoB on the day the petition for sequestration was presented;
- in the case of a petition by a creditor, the requirements of the 1985 Act relating to apparent insolvency have been fulfilled; and
- in the case of a petition by a trustee, the averments in his petition as to any of the conditions in s 5(2C) of the 1985 Act are true.

Where all of the above criteria are fulfilled, the sheriff must award sequestration and the case of *Sales Lease Ltd v Minty* (1993) demonstrates that the sheriff has no discretion in the matter. However, in terms of s 12(3B) of the 1985 Act, the sheriff has the power to continue the petition for a period of no more than 42 days where the sheriff is satisfied that the debtor shall, before the expiry of the period of 42 days beginning with the day on which the debtor appears before the sheriff, pay or satisfy the debt in respect of which the debtor became apparently insolvent and any other debt due by the debtor to the petitioner and any creditor concurring in the petition.

The date of sequestration

The date of the sheriff's warrant to cite the debtor is critical. It is the "date of sequestration" where sequestration is awarded on the presentation of a petition for sequestration before the sheriff. Section 14 of the 1985 Act, which is very important, stipulates that registration of (1) the court order (in a case where the sheriff has awarded sequestration subsequent to the presentation of a petition) or (2) the AoB's determination of the debtor application awarding sequestration, must be made in the Register of Inhibitions. Moreover, a copy of the court order must be sent to the AoB and any Debt Arrangement Scheme Administrator appointed under the Debt Arrangement and Attachment (Scotland) Act 2002.

Sheriff's or AoB's refusal to award sequestration

Where the sheriff decides to refuse the award of sequestration, the petitioner or a concurring creditor may lodge an appeal against that decision in terms of s 15(3) of the 1985 Act. Likewise, where the AoB refuses to award sequestration pursuant to a debtor application, the debtor may appeal to the sheriff in accordance with s 15(3A) of the 1985 Act.

Recall of award of sequestration

Where the AoB or the sheriff decides to award sequestration, it is not possible to appeal that decision. However, the 1985 Act prescribes a procedure in terms of s 16 which enables the debtor, any creditor, the AoB, the trustee in sequestration or other interested person to present a petition for recall of the sequestration to the sheriff. The sheriff has the power to recall the sequestration in terms of s 17(1) of the 1985 Act if he is satisfied that it is appropriate to do so taking into account all the circumstances of the case, including matters arising after sequestration and certain factors listed in s 17(2) of the 1985 Act.

Effect of appointment of trustee in sequestration

Where the trustee in sequestration is appointed, a decree of appointment is made which has effect in accordance with ss 31, 32 and 33 of the 1985 Act. These are crucially important sections, since they stipulate the assets of the debtor which vest in and can be dealt with by the trustee. Section 31(1) of the 1985 Act directs quite clearly that the effect of the trustee's appointment is to vest the debtor's whole estate in the trustee of sequestration as at the date of sequestration for the benefit of the debtor's creditors. Thus, s 31 of the 1985 Act essentially provides for the statutory conveyance of the entirety of the debtor's assets in the trustee. However, this statutory transfer in title is subject to the *tantum et tale* rule which means that defects in the title of the debtor pass on to the trustee and the trustee can inherit no better title to the debtor's assets than the debtor had himself (*Heritable Reversionary Co Ltd* v *Millar* (1892)). Thus, if the debtor's property was subject to some encumbrance, eg a lease, the trustee takes title to the asset subject to that lease.

Exceptions to statutory transfer of debtor's assets

28-day handicap for heritage

The 1985 Act provides for various exceptions to the general rule that the trustee takes the entire estate of the debtor on the appointment of the trustee in sequestration. In particular, with regard to the heritable property of the debtor, s 31(1A) and (1B) of the 1985 Act narrate that the trustee in sequestration is subject to a handicap in perfecting title to the heritable property of the debtor. It is provided that the trustee will not be able to register title to the debtor's heritage for a period of 28 days beginning with the date of registration of the notice registered in the Register of Inhibitions in accordance with s 14 of the 1985 Act. The 28-day handicap rule was introduced by the 2007 Act to offset the effects of *Burnett's Trustee* v *Grainger* (2004). In *Burnett's Trustee*, a trustee in sequestration registered a notice of title to the debtor's heritable property after his appointment. The date of registration of that notice of title preceded the date on which a third-party purchaser (who had paid the purchase price to the debtor) from the debtor had registered a disposition of property belonging to the debtor. The prior registration of that notice of title was sufficient to defeat the rights of the third-party purchaser (even though the latter had paid the purchase price to the debtor prior to the date of sequestration), since the trustee had won the "race to the register". The 28-day rule seeks to ensure that a purchaser of heritable property from the debtor prior to the date of sequestration has a period of 28 days to register its disposition from the date of registration of the court order of the sequestration of the debtor in the Register of Inhibitions.

Corporeal moveables

Section 31(4) of the 1985 Act directs that where delivery, possession or intimation would normally be required to complete the trustee's title to moveables, such delivery, possession or intimation will be deemed to have occurred by operation of law. However, in the case of incorporeal moveables, where some further step is necessary to perfect title, eg registration in the register of members of a company or the UK Intellectual Property Office in the case of shares or patents respectively, completion of the trustee's title to those assets does not take place until the occurrence of that step (*Cumming's Tr* v *Glenrinnes Farms Ltd* (1993)). The consequence of this rule is that the trustee's rights may be defeated where a third party registers title to the property before the trustee (*Morrison* v *Harrison* (1876)). Moreover, on the vesting of the debtor's moveable assets in the trustee in sequestration, any rights to payment relating to such corporeal moveable assets are also acquired by the trustee, eg a right to be paid rent or hire payments (*Mitchell's Trs* v *Pearson* (1834)). In the case of obligations relating to the moveable assets of the debtor, those obligations are not transferred to the trustee, eg a tenant's obligations in terms of a lease. The general rule is that the trustee in sequestration has the option whether to choose to assume those obligations by adopting the contract or not (see s 42(1) of the 1985 Act and *MacDonald's Trs* v *Cunningham* (1987)).

Acquirenda

With regard to a*cquirenda*, ie assets or rights acquired by the debtor after the date of sequestration but before his discharge, s 32(6) of the 1985 Act specifically provides that any person who holds any such estate must convey or deliver it to the trustee. A common example is where a debtor inherits assets or money from a third party. Likewise, free shares issued by a company are deemed to be *acquirenda* in terms of the case of *Accountant in Bankruptcy* v *Halifax plc* (1999) and so vest in the trustee. However, s 32(6) of the Act provides an exception whereby where a person has in good faith and without knowledge of the sequestration conveyed the estate to the debtor or to a third party on the instructions of the debtor, that person incurs no liability to the trustee except to account for any proceeds of the conveyance which are in his hands. Where a third party conveys property or assets to the debtor in circumstances where he is aware of the debtor's sequestration, the case of *Rankin's Trs* v *H C Somerville & Russell* (1999) is to the effect that the trustee has the right to seek a remedy against that third party, and if the property paid by the third party to the debtor is cash, the trustee's remedy will be to raise a money claim.

Income

The treatment of the debtor's income is governed by s 32(1) of the 1985 Act which stipulates that any income which is received by the debtor after the date of sequestration vests in the debtor and does not pass to the trustee. However, there is an exception. Where income generated is derived from estate vested in the trustee, that income transfers to the trustee, eg rents which are derived from moveable or heritable property which has vested in the trustee. The case of *Accountant in Bankruptcy* v *Halifax plc* (1999) decided that free shares issued to the debtor are *acquirenda* and not income and so vest in the trustee. Meanwhile, estate of the debtor which is located outside Scotland does not vest in the trustee.

Trust assets and other assets

Property which is held in trust by the debtor does not vest in the trustee as a result of s 33(1)(b) of the 1985 Act. Implicit within this rule is the recognition that the debtor's estate may be divided into his personal patrimony and trust patrimony. Section 122 of the Social Security Contributions and Benefits Act 1992 and ss 187 and 191 of the Social Security Administration Act 1992 also exclude social security payments from vesting in the trustee. Such payments are treated as if they are inalienable and the rights to such payments remain with the debtor. Meanwhile, certain property is exempt from vesting in terms of s 33(1)(a) of the 1985 Act. Section 33(1)(a) of the 1985 Act refers to items which are excluded from the diligence of attachment in s 11 of, and Sch 2 to, the Debt Arrangement and Attachment (Scotland) Act 2002. Such items include the debtor's books, implements, tools of trade or other equipment required for the exercise of his practice or profession, subject to an aggregate maximum of £1,000.

Duties and functions of trustee in sequestration

The key duties and functions of the trustee in sequestration are set out in ss 3, 39 and 49 of the 1985 Act. The trustee's duties can be divided into two categories. First, the trustee is under an obligation to recover, manage and realise the estate of the debtor. Secondly, once the trustee has realised a pot of money, the trustee must then distribute those funds among the debtor's creditors according to a statutorily prescribed order. In distributing such funds, s 51(6) of the 1985 Act states that secured creditors will be the first persons to be paid by the trustee to the extent that they are entitled to receive the value of their security before the estate is distributed in accordance with the rules in the 1985 Act. Thereafter, the trustee must apply the proceeds of the debtor's estate towards payment of his outlays and remuneration. In the case of deceased debtors, the funeral expenses are paid out next. Thereafter, the expenses of the creditor who petitioned for sequestration must be paid followed by sums owed to the preferred creditors. Preferred debts include the accrued holiday pay of employees of the debtor up to the date of sequestration (eg where the debtor is a sole trader) and arrears of wages of the debtor's employees up to 4 months before the sequestration date subject to a ceiling of £800 per employee. Once such preferred creditors have been paid, ordinary unsecured creditors are paid and then interest on debts is paid. Finally, postponed creditors are paid.

It is unusual for all ordinary unsecured creditors to be paid in full. It is common for such ordinary unsecured creditors to be paid a percent-age of their claim. In such circumstances, each of the ordinary unsecured creditors ranks *pari passu*, ie they rank equally where there are insufficient funds to pay each of them in full. A final point to stress is that s 32 of the 1985 Act provides that a proportion of the bankrupt debtor's income which he receives after he has been discharged as a bankrupt can nevertheless be taken for payment to the creditors.

Discharge of debtor

Once the debtor's estate has been applied to pay off the creditors, the debtor is discharged and is relieved from any continuing liability to his creditors. This rule holds good even in those circumstances where creditors have not received the full extent of the sums which they were due to be paid or where the sequestration continues and the trustee remains in office. It is important to stress that debtors are automatically discharged from sequestration on the first anniversary of the date of sequestration by virtue of s 54(1) of the 1985 Act. However, s 54(3) enables the trustee or any creditor of the debtor to apply to the sheriff to defer the automatic discharge for a further period of 2 years in circumstances where the debtor has not co-operated with the trustee in the sequestration. Moreover, the discharge of the debtor does not automatically reinvest him in his property. However, the debtor has the right to acquire assets subsequent to his discharge.

CHALLENGES TO PRIOR TRANSACTIONS

Where the debtor enters into a transaction with a third party prior to his insolvency, the trustee in sequestration may challenge that transaction by recovering any assets transferred to third parties and/or strike down any rights in security granted in favour of third parties. Such prior transactions are known as "challengeable transactions" and may be pursued in terms of the common law or the provisions of the 1985 Act. However, consideration of the law of challengeable transactions will be restricted here to the provisions contained in the 1985 Act. There are two types of challengeable transaction under the 1985 Act. It is important to stress that such a prior transaction can be challenged only where a trustee in sequestration has established that the debtor is absolutely insolvent, ie that the debtor's total liabilities exceed his total assets (s 73(2) of the 1985 Act) (so that the debtor is balance sheet insolvent).

Gratuitous alienations

The first challengeable transaction is known as a "gratuitous alienation" and is governed by s 34 of the 1985 Act. It is a gift or part gift of property or money by the debtor to a third party. If the debtor is absolutely insolvent, the trustee in sequestration, a judicial factor, a creditor of the debtor, or a trustee under a trust deed all have the power to challenge the gratuitous alienation. Where the trustee in sequestration decides not to take action under s 34 of the 1985 Act, the case of *Accountant in Bankruptcy* v *Brown* (2009) directs that a creditor may nevertheless pursue a third party in accordance with the provisions in the 1985 Act on gratuitous alienations. There is no requirement for the trustee or creditors to demonstrate that the debtor sought to defraud his creditors or that the alienation was entered into with a view to avoiding the effects of bankruptcy.

Criteria for establishment of gratuitous alienation

Section 34 of the 1985 Act directs that there must be an alienation by the debtor. Secondly, the alienation must involve the transfer of the property or funds of the debtor or renounce or discharge a debtor's claim or right against a third party. Thirdly, (a) the debtor must have been sequestrated, (b) the debtor must have been granted a trust deed for behoof of his creditors, or (c) a judicial factor must have been appointed over the estate of the debtor. Fourthly, the alienation must have occurred within the periods stipulated in the 1985 Act. The relevant period is 5 years before the date of sequestration, the grant of the trust deed or the appointment of the judicial factor, where the debtor transfers his property or money to a third party who is an associate of the debtor. An associate is defined by s 74 of the 1985 Act as someone that is the husband, wife, civil partner, partner (in the sense of a business partnership), employee, employer, brother, sister, uncle, aunt, nephew, niece or other relative of the debtor. However, in all other cases where property is transferred, the appropriate period is 2 years before the relevant date of sequestration, the grant of the trust deed or the appointment of the judicial factor.

The relevant date of alienation

The relevant date for the purposes of determining when the alienation took place is governed by section 34(3) of the 1985 Act. The relevant date is when the alienation became completely effectual. The case of *Craiglaw Developments Ltd* v *Wilson* (1997) decided that the date of alienation in the case of the transfer of moveables is the date of their delivery. In the context of the conveyance of heritage, the cases of *Grant's Tr* v *Grant* (1986) and *Accountant in Bankruptcy* v *Orr* (2005) demonstrate that the relevant date is the recording of the purchaser's disposition in the Register of Sasines.

Third party defences

Where the trustee in sequestration or creditor challenges the alienation to the third party, the third party who is seeking to uphold the validity of the alienation has certain defences under s 34(4) of the 1985 Act. The first defence under s 34(4)(a) of the 1985 Act is to the effect that the debtor's liabilities did not exceed his assets, ie the debtor was not absolutely insolvent. The second defence in s 34(4)(b) of the 1985 Act permits the third party to uphold the alienation where he can demonstrate that it was for adequate consideration. The final defence open to the third party is that the alienation was a permitted gift. Section 34(4)(c) of the 1985 Act specifies that a birthday gift, Christmas gift, other conventional gift or a charitable gift (not to an associate) are covered, provided that it was reasonable for the debtor to make those gifts having regard to all the circumstances.

"Adequate consideration"

In practice, it is the second defence which features most heavily in the reported cases, ie that the alienation was given for adequate consideration. This begs the question as to what constitutes "adequate consideration"?

In the case of *MacFadyen's Tr* v *MacFadyen* (1994), a mother had purchased a property for her son and she met the running costs of the property. The title to the property was transferred subsequently by the son to the mother for no consideration. When the son became bankrupt, the mother and son sought to uphold the alienation on the basis that the purchase price which she had paid and her contribution to the running costs amounted to adequate consideration. The court disagreed and ruled that the word "consideration" meant something which was given or surrendered in return for something else and had to be something of material or patrimonial value which could be vindicated in a legal process at the time when it was given. On that basis, it was held that the purchase price and the running costs pre-dated the alienation and so could not amount to adequate consideration. A similar case is *Cay's Trs* v *Cay* (1998) which held that a husband's obligation to aliment his wife could not represent adequate consideration.

Remedies

Where an action challenging a gratuitous alienation is successful, various remedies are available. Section 34(4) of the 1985 Act stipulates that the court must grant a decree of reduction, a decree restoring the property alienated to the debtor's estate or a decree in respect of such "other redress as may be appropriate". But where a third party has acquired the property in good faith and for value, s 34(3) of the 1985 Act states that such person will not be prejudiced. On the face of it, it is unclear what is meant by such "other redress as may be appropriate" in s 34(3) of the 1985 Act. However, guidance is provided by the case of *Short's Tr* v *Chung* (1991), where it was held that such words did not provide the court with a general discretion as to remedies. An order other than reduction or restoration of the property is available only where those two remedies are unavailable.

Unfair preferences

The other transaction which may be challenged by a trustee in sequestration, a judicial factor, a creditor of the debtor or a trustee under a trust deed is referred to as an "unfair preference" and is governed by s 36 of the 1985 Act. Section 36 of the Act prohibits a debtor from preferring one creditor over other creditors since it represents a violation of the debtor's duty to treat creditors equally and fairly. Like the law of gratuitous alienations, unfair preferences can be challenged on the basis of the common law or s 36 of the 1985 Act. Section 36 of the 1985 Act directs that a preference which is created in favour of a creditor within 6 months of the date of sequestration of the debtor or the date when the debtor grants a trust deed for behoof of creditors can be struck down by the court. Preferences include the situation where a debtor pays one creditor before other creditors, grants a security in favour of a particular creditor (but not the other creditors), provides assistance to a particular creditor (but not the other creditors) in executing diligence over the debtor's assets or where the debtor enters into a sham sale of moveable property while retaining possession. For obvious reasons, the first example given is the most common in practice, eg where a debtor arranges to pay a particular favourite creditor even though the date of that creditor's invoice or fee post-dates the invoices or fees of other creditors. Like gratuitous alienations, s 36(3) of the 1985 Act is to the effect that a preference will be deemed to have been created on the date it became effectual.

Excluded transactions

Certain transactions may not be challenged by the trustee, creditor or judicial factor. First, where the debtor enters into a transaction in the ordinary course of trade or business and the creditor is not influenced by any belief that the debtor might be insolvent (see s 36(2)(a) and *Nordic Travel Ltd* v *Scotprint Ltd* (1980)). Secondly, any transaction involving the payment of cash (including banknotes, bankers' drafts, cheques, coins and bills) where there is no collusion between the debtor and the creditor (eg where the creditor is aware of the debtor's precarious financial position and arranges payment in order to defeat the interests of the other creditors of the debtor). Finally, any transaction which represents *nova debita* is excluded, ie where the debtor and creditor are bound by reciprocal obligations.

Remedies

The remedies available to the successful trustee, creditor or judicial factor are reduction, restoration and such other redress as may be appropriate.

Essential Facts

- There are three types of insolvency, namely practical insolvency, absolute insolvency and apparent insolvency.
- Sequestration describes the process whereby the assets of an insolvent debtor are sold and the proceeds of sale are distributed amongst his creditors.
- The trustee in sequestration administers a debtor's estate on sequestration of that debtor.
- The process of sequestration may be initiated by a creditor or other qualified parties presenting a petition to the sheriff court or by debtor application procedure.
- The effect of the trustee in sequestration's appointment is to vest the debtor's whole estate in the trustee as at the date of sequestration for the benefit of the debtor's creditors.
- Certain assets of the debtor are excluded from vesting in terms of the 1985 Act.
- A trustee in sequestration or creditor may challenge certain transactions entered into by the debtor prior to sequestration on the basis that they constitute a gratuitous alienation or an unfair preference.

Essential Cases

Sales Lease Ltd v Minty (1993): where the criteria in s 12(3) of the 1985 Act are satisfied the sheriff must grant an award of sequestration and has no discretion in the matter.

Heritable Reversionary Co Ltd v Millar (1892): on the statutory conveyance of title to the debtor's estate to the trustee pursuant to s 32(6) of the 1985 Act, any defects in the title of the debtor pass on to the trustee and the trustee can inherit no better title to the debtor's assets than the debtor had himself.

Cumming's Tr v Glenrinnes Farms Ltd (1993) and **Morrison v Harrison (1876)**: in the case of incorporeal moveable assets such as shares and patents which require some other step such as registration to perfect title, the trustee's rights may be defeated where a third party registers title to the property before the trustee.

Accountant in Bankruptcy v Halifax plc (1999): bonus shares issued by a company are deemed to be *acquirenda* and not income of the debtor, so they vest in the trustee.

Rankin's Trs v H C Somerville & Russell (1999): where a third party conveys property or assets to the debtor in circumstances where he is aware of the debtor's sequestration, the trustee has a right of recourse against that third party.

Accountant in Bankruptcy v Brown (2009): where the trustee in sequestration decides not to challenge a gratuitous alienation, a creditor may nevertheless pursue a third party under the 1985 Act.

Craiglaw Developments Ltd v Wilson (1997): the date of alienation for the purposes of s 34(3) of the 1985 Act in the case of the transfer of moveables is the date of their delivery.

Accountant in Bankruptcy v Orr (2005): the date of alienation for the purposes of s 34(3) of the 1985 Act in the case of the transfer of heritage is the date of recording of the purchaser's disposition in the Register of Sasines.

MacFadyen's Tr v MacFadyen (1994): "consideration" in s 34(4)(b) of the 1985 Act means something which was given or surrendered in return for something else and had to be something of material or patrimonial value which could be vindicated in a legal process at the time when it was given.

Cay's Trs v Cay (1998): a husband's obligation to aliment his wife could not amount to adequate consideration.

12 COMMERCIAL DISPUTE RESOLUTION

In previous chapters, the various rights and obligations which are enjoyed and owed by parties in commercial and consumer transactions have been charted. Where disputes arise between seller and purchaser, insured and insurer, owner and hirer, etc, about those rights and obligations, litigation in court is available as a means of resolving that dispute. However, it is not the only avenue which is available. The parties may opt to resolve their disputes through a process other than litigation in the courts. It is the purpose of this chapter to provide an exposition of the various dispute resolution mechanisms which are available.

SUMMARY OF PRINCIPAL FORMS OF DISPUTE RESOLUTION PROCESS

The most obvious option for a person seeking to enforce a legal right is to take legal action in the courts, ie to litigate. The courts are the principal avenue provided by the legal system as a means of enabling a party to vindicate his legal rights. An alternative is for a party to seek to enforce his legal rights through arbitration. Unlike litigation, arbitration is not conducted in a public forum and so for that reason possesses many attractions. However, arbitration is similar to litigation in the sense that the parties may lead evidence and call witnesses before a third party known as the arbiter. Moreover, in the cases of litigation and arbitration, a decision which is legally binding is handed down by a third party (ie the judge in the case of litigation and the arbiter in the case of arbitration).

Other forms of dispute resolution procedure involve the parties in dispute receiving a legally binding decision. The most important in the context of commercial law is neutral expert/neutral evaluation and mediation/conciliation. In the case of a neutral expert procedure, the parties submit their dispute to a nominated expert for resolution. The parties commonly opt into this procedure in terms of a contractual provision and it is particularly common for them to do so in circumstances where property such as land, buildings, shares or intellectual property rights requires to be valued and there is a dispute between the parties as to the correct figure. Where an expert is appointed, the expert applies his expertise, skill and experience to fix the valuation. Meanwhile, mediation/

conciliation is an altogether different dispute resolution process and entails the mediator/conciliator operating in a role as facilitator, concentrating on bringing the parties in dispute towards consensus and resolution. The mediator/conciliator may take an active role in highlighting the strengths and weaknesses in each party's case or may adopt a less intrusive role. Much depends on the context of the dispute and the nature of the training undertaken by the mediator/conciliator. This chapter examines litigation and arbitration only.

LITIGATION

Introduction and disadvantages

Litigation is conducted in the courts of law which are constituted by the legal system. Some of the characteristics of litigation operate as disadvantages in the commercial arena. First, the fact that litigation is conducted in the public arena is a particular drawback since commercial organisations will usually be keen to avoid information which is detrimental to their reputation becoming publicly available. It may be damaging to commercial interests for that information to be made public. Secondly, litigation is usually costly. Thirdly, litigation generally takes a long time to be completed, and during that period, the commercial relationship between the parties may be irretrievably damaged to the point where they are no longer in a position to continue trading with each other. Sometimes this will not be a concern but it will be particularly disadvantageous where there are few alternative traders in the market. Another difficulty with litigation is that, once it has been completed, it will resolve the legal issue which has resulted in the dispute, but it will do nothing to resolve all other commercial issues which may exist between the parties.

Remedies

Before a party engages in litigation, he must be absolutely clear as to the remedy which he is seeking. The remedies available through the courts are count, reckoning and payment (ie a decree ordering someone to pay a debt), damages (ie a decree ordering someone to pay compensation in respect of a person's loss), declarator (a decree which declares a particular state of affairs to exist), specific implement (a decree compelling someone to do something), interdict (a decree compelling someone not to do something) and reduction (a decree denuding a deed or other legal document of legal effect). Moreover, only a court has the power to grant a party diligence on the dependence of an action, inhibition and reduction. Litigation is an option which is always available to the parties in order to enforce their rights. However, this can be contrasted with arbitration which is only an option where the parties have contracted into arbitration in terms of a contractual agreement.

The courts and procedures

In Scotland, commercial disputes may be litigated in the sheriff court or the Court of Session.

Sheriff court

Litigation may be pursued in the sheriff court pursuant to ordinary cause or summary cause procedures. Ordinary actions involve the service of an initial writ on the defender in terms of rule 3.1 of the Act of Sederunt (Sheriff Court Ordinary Cause Rules) 1993 (SI 1993/1956) ("Ordinary Cause Rules") whereby the defender has 21 days to respond. If the defender fails to provide such a response, the pursuer will be entitled to a decree in absence in terms of rule 7 of the Ordinary Cause Rules. The summary cause procedure enables the pursuer to seek an amount between £3,000 and £5,000 in terms of rule 4 of the Act of Sederunt (Summary Cause Rules) 2002 (SSI 2002/132). Another form of procedure which is similar to the summary cause procedure and which may be pursued in the sheriff court is the small claims procedure. A pursuer may raise a civil action pursuant to the small claims procedure in terms of the Small Claims (Scotland) Order 1988 (SI 1988/1999) as amended by the Small Claims (Scotland) Amendment Order 2007 (SSI 2007/496). A civil action may be raised through the small claims procedure where the claim is for an amount of no more than £3,000. The small claims procedure envisages that the pursuer will represent himself. However, it is not wholly unusual for pursuers to be represented by qualified legal practitioners. As a result, the sheriff commonly takes a more active role in small claims proceedings.

Court of Session

Where a case is factually or legally complex, it is not uncommon for the pursuer to initiate a claim in the Court of Session. A case can be brought before the Court of Session only where the value of the claim is £5,000 or more, in terms of ss 31 and 35 of the Sheriff Courts (Scotland) Act

1971. The procedures for initiating action in the Court of Session are governed by the Court of Session rules set out in the Act of Sederunt (Rules of the Court of Session) 1994 (SI 1994/1443). The Court of Session action is raised by the pursuer preparing a document called a summons in the prescribed form. The summons is then signeted if the requisite fee is paid and it meets the requirements of form. Once the summons is signetted, it will be served on the defender. After a period of 21 days, the summons may be lodged with the court for calling and the defender has a short period of 3 days to notify the court that he intends to defend the action by appearing to contest it. The defender has 7 days from the date the summons is called to submit written defences to the court. The defences are then served upon the pursuer and the pursuer has a period of 14 days to lodge the open record within 14 days of the date when the defences were lodged. The open record is then adjusted by the pursuer and the defender over a period of 8 weeks. After the period of 8 weeks, the record is closed and the pursuer then has a further period of 4 weeks to lodge the closed record. The closed record is the document which draws the summons and the defences together in one document and thus sets out the pleadings of both of the parties to the dispute. The court will fix a proof (a process whereby witnesses and evidence are led), fix a proof before answer (a process whereby witnesses and evidence are led and the case involves a point of law) or schedule a debate on a point of law (which is based on the pleadings in the closed record and in the absence of witnesses and evidence).

Where the subject of the dispute is a matter of commercial law, a specialised commercial action may be raised in the Court of Session. Rule 47.1.2 of the Court of Session Rules directs that a commercial action is an action arising out of, or concerned with, any transaction or dispute of a commercial or business nature. The action does not require to be based on a contract and may include a dispute about leases, construction matters, contracts of sale, insurance, hire-purchase contracts, financial services and other listed matters. The onus falls on the pursuer to seek to have their action dealt with under the commercial action procedure and they may do so by labelling the action as a commercial action in the summons. In a commercial action, the judge plays a very pro-active role in managing the case and is entitled to make a variety of orders. Moreover, the judge is carefully appointed and will commonly have experience in commercial law matters. For that reason, the commercial action procedure is particularly attractive to commercial organisations which are in dispute.

ARBITRATION

Introduction

In Scotland, there are two forms of arbitration. There is the domestic law of arbitration which is based principally on the common law with some statutory additions. Secondly, the UNCITRAL Model Law on International Commercial Arbitration ("the Model Law") applies to international commercial arbitrations which take place in Scotland. The Model Law applies where one of the parties is not based in Scotland and was introduced into Scots law by virtue of s 66 of, and Sch 7 to, the Law Reform (Miscellaneous Provisions) (Scotland) Act 1990. This chapter considers the domestic law of arbitration only.

Advantages of arbitration

One of the main benefits of arbitration is that a party has the capacity to appoint as an arbiter a person who is an expert in the field of the particular commercial dispute. Moreover, arbitration may be less expensive than litigation and is private. The procedure is more flexible than court procedure and the resolution of the dispute may be brought to a swifter conclusion. In addition, it may be more straightforward to enforce an arbitral award in a foreign jurisdiction than a court decree from a Scottish court.

Reference of matters to arbitration

The parties may refer disputes between themselves to arbitration in terms of a contract. The agreement may be contained in the original contract between the parties or in terms of an arbitration agreement once a dispute arises between them. If the parties agree to resolve their dispute by arbitration, the courts will enforce that agreement (*Sanderson* v *Armour & Co* (1922)). If one of the parties subsequently attempts to litigate the dispute in the courts, the courts will refuse to hear the matter and will refer it to arbitration.

Conduct of proceedings

The nature of the proceedings and their conduct will be governed by the arbitration agreement or the original contract. If the agreement fails to set down the proceedings, the arbiter will decide the procedure to be followed (*Holmes Oil Co v Pumpherston Oil Co* (1890)). For example, the arbiter will determine whether written claims and defences ought to be placed before the arbitration and whether witnesses and other evidence should be heard.

The stated case procedure

When an arbiter resolves a dispute, the common law provided that this was determinative of the fact and law of the dispute in question. However, s 3(1) of the Administration of Justice (Scotland) Act 1972 now permits the parties to state a case for the opinion of the Court of Session in respect of any question of law arising from the dispute. The effect of this provision is that the parties may effectively appeal any legal issue which arises from the arbiter's decision. The parties may oust their entitlement in s 3(1) of the Administration of Justice (Scotland) Act 1972 to refer any legal issue to the Court of Session by stated case procedure. Contracting out can be achieved in an arbitration agreement or the original contract (*Whatlings (Foundations) Ltd* v *Shanks & McEwan (Contractors) Ltd* (1989)). A stated case can only be taken forward to the Court of Session on the application of one of the parties to the dispute. However, it can only be raised at any stage of the arbitration proceedings. Therefore, once the proceedings have ended and the arbiter has made his award, it is too late for a stated case to be made (*Fairlie Yacht Slip* v *Lumsden* (1977)).

The award

Once the arbiter has considered the dispute, he will produce an arbitral award. In practice, the arbiter will usually deliver the award in draft. This enables the parties to state a case to the Court of Session on a point of law. An award may interdict a party, declare the rights of the parties (similar to a court declarator) or grant specific implement. However, it is not possible to award damages.

Essential Facts

- The courts are the principal avenue provided by the legal system as a means of enabling a party to vindicate his legal rights.
- Arbitration, neutral expert/neutral evaluation and mediation/conciliation are alternative means of resolving commercial disputes.
- Litigation may take place in the sheriff courts or the Court of Session.

- There are two recognised forms of arbitration in Scots law, namely the common law and the Model Law.
- Section 3(1) of the Administration of Justice (Scotland) Act 1972 permits parties in dispute to state a case for the opinion of the Court of Session in respect of any question of law arising from the arbitration, ie to appeal an arbiter's decision on a point of law.

Essential Cases

Sanderson v Armour & Co (1922): where the parties have agreed to resolve any disputes arising between them by arbitration, or one of the parties subsequently attempts to litigate the dispute in the courts, the courts will refuse to hear the matter and will refer it to arbitration.

Holmes Oil Co v Pumpherston Oil Co (1890): if the agreement fails to clarify the conduct of the proceedings of the arbitration, the arbiter will decide the procedure to be followed.

Whatlings (Foundations) Ltd v Shanks & McEwan (Contractors) Ltd (1989): the parties may contract out of s 3(1) of the Administration of Justice (Scotland) Act 1972 by stipulating this in an arbitration agreement or the original contract

Fairlie Yacht Slip v Lumsden (1977): once arbitration proceedings have ended and the arbiter has produced his award, a stated case may not be made to the Court of Session.

INDEX